Television:
A GUIDE
FOR CHRISTIANS

Television:
A GUIDE
FOR CHRISTIANS

Ed McNulty

Abingdon
Nashville

Television: A GUIDE FOR CHRISTIANS

Copyright © 1976 by Abingdon

Library of Congress Cataloging in Publication Data

McNulty, Edward N., 1936-
 Television, a guide for Christians.

 Bibliography: p. 94
 1. Television in religion. I. Title.
BV656.3.M3   268'.635   76-1990

ISBN 0-687-41220-X

Scripture quotations are from the Revised Standard Version
of the Bible copyrighted 1946, 1952, and 1971, by the Division
of Christian Education, National Council of Churches, and
are used by permission.

Permission to use the text of the radio spot on page 48 was
granted by United Methodist Communications, New York,
New York.

The Peanuts and Grinch questions on page 62 originally
appeared in *Update,* November 1974, of *Thesis Theological
Cassettes.*

MANUFACTURED BY THE PARTHENON PRESS AT
NASHVILLE, TENNESSEE, UNITED STATES OF AMERICA

For Sandra

Contents

Introduction

This is not a television production book, but a guide to help the average intelligent Christian watch television more critically, and to have more fun while doing it. Marshall McLuhan stated that he wrote so much about television hoping that people would kick it in its antennae. That is, he wanted them to be aware of their electronic environment and thus be able to act upon it and not just be acted upon by it.

My purpose is not so much to kick TV in its antennae—though parts of the book are critical of the medium—as to help people enjoy it more while examining their faith. This is a book about the gospel as much as it is about TV. Many people, especially church leaders, have been critical of television, and rightly so. There are some moments when you do become angry at the vast amount of trash that lights up our tubes. But my contention is that even the trash can be used effectively in a Christian education program—and that's why the first type of programming covered in this book is the soap opera. Even a commercial can be used as a way of exploring aspects of the Sermon on the Mount if you know how to go about it. I hope this book will give you some ideas on this.

The *Guide* can be used by groups with limited time, such

Introduction

as church school classes, or by those with a large amount of time, such as retreat groups, evening study groups, or schools and conferences. Even a quick glance will show you that this is not a collection of essays *about* TV, but a series of probes, questions, and exercises designed to get you *into* TV and the gospel. Although some people might enjoy reading it alone, it is really meant to be used as a resource for a group study.

The first part of each Channel (what else could we call the chapters of such a book?) contains the basic material a group with limited time should plan to cover. This section, depending on the Channel, will take from one to three hours to cover. Thus the leader will want to plan each session carefully and not feel compelled to cover everything. You might also find portions of the second section, "Further Probes," which will interest your group. Feel free to substitute or add these. However, since these sections usually probe more deeply, you may want to use them toward the end of your session. You might want to spend two or three meetings on some Channels, one on another, and perhaps none on a topic that simply leaves you cold. The third part of each Channel, the contem-

porary worship services, contains seed ideas for groups at retreats or conferences who want to celebrate their involvement in media.

The "And Now a Word from . . ." segments are intended to stimulate thought and discussion. Some are written with tongue in cheek. In some, pertinent information is given. Others contain theological insights, or relevant ideas from the scriptures related to the subject. Most of them have been kept short to follow the TV format. In fact, when read aloud, they will fill about sixty seconds, the time of many commercials. The group leader is urged to record these on a cassette tape ahead of time and play them back for the group at the designated places in each session.

The leader's task will be to gather the people, prepare the materials for each session, make assignments, start the meeting, and keep the group more or less on the track. When time is limited, the leader may have to pick which of the questions and activities are to be included, at least for the first session or two. After the initial session, the group might want to help make this kind of decision. If everyone has a copy of the book, leading the discussion should be easy and could be shared on a

Introduction

rotating basis. Whatever the method used, the leader will have to read ahead in order to make assignments and preparations for the next session. There should be a wide enough variety of questions and projects so that any group, from junior high youth to older adults, can have an enjoyable learning experience with the book.

A group that is already into television might want to skip "Sign On," since it seeks to orient the group to television in a general way. Remember, this is a guide, so don't feel you have to follow every suggestion slavishly.

The best way to use this book is while gathered around the TV set. This may mean meeting at unusual times in order to catch particular programs suitable for the session. However, the book can be used in settings where this is not possible, such as a camp or a retreat center. If a TV set is not available or the reception is poor, the leader might ask a task group to video tape certain programs and bring the tape deck and monitor to camp. This is no longer an impossible dream since many local denominational offices now own video equipment. Some schools and educational centers are willing to loan or rent theirs, especially on weekends.

Another alternative is to ask various group members to tape the audio portion of programs and to make notes on the video portion. As a last resort (but one that may prove surprisingly effective) group members can rely on their memories and describe various shows they have seen. In all cases, copies of *TV Guide* magazine will be an invaluable help.

Your basic tools will be a TV set, Bibles (any version, though the Revised Standard Version is quoted mostly in this book), *TV Guide* magazines, a cassette tape recorder, one copy of this book for each participant, pencils, and paper. Other materials for the creative projects and worship celebrations are suggested in each Channel. Most of all, you need some spirited, inquiring folk willing to explore the gospel through electronic media—and electronic media through the gospel. This book does not attempt to cover every area of TV programming, but it can give you the tools and encouragement to go on and explore other aspects on your own.

I have discovered what other authors have maintained, that the writing of books is not just a private affair, but a process

Introduction

in which many folk are involved. This is true for this book in particular, and so I want to express my appreciation to Dennis Benson for getting me started on this project; Marilyn Benson for looking through several chapters and making helpful suggestions; Jim and Judy Culberson for gathering a group at my former parish to try out two of the chapters; the adults from Bethel Presbyterian Church who met for a run-through of "Sign On"; my children for giving up family time so that I could write this—and for many hours of watching and talking about television together; and most of all Sandy, my life companion, for her encouragement, for undertaking the tedious task of typing the manuscript, for making a myriad of corrections, and for suggestions to clarify obscure passages.

Such folk Paul must have had in mind when he wrote to the Philippians, "I thank my God in all my remembrance of you, always in every prayer of mine for you all making my prayer with joy, thankful for your partnership in the gospel."

Edward McNulty

SIGN ON

"And Now a Word from . . ."

You are invited to journey into the world of television—not the world of cameras and lights at a studio, but the world created in your own living room or den by the often lit tube bringing in its hours of entertainment and information. This little book can guide you in exploring the implications and values of television, especially as they might relate to the Christian gospel. You might not have seen much connection between TV and the gospel, except for the times when Billy Graham was televising a rally; but there is more to TV than meets the eye.

For the Leader

Have on hand: Bibles (any translation), TV set, cassette tape and recorder, copies of this book for all group members, several copies of *TV Guide* magazine, paper, and pencils.

Start this session with whatever preliminary remarks and suggestions you need to make, then play your cassette recording of the "And Now a Word from . . ." section, and jump into the questions. If the members have had the book in advance, you can keep your introductory remarks brief and to the point. Pass out Bibles and copies of *TV Guide*.

Sign On

For the Group

1. Why do you watch television? How is watching TV different from going to a movie, reading a book, or attending a sports event?

2. Look over your copy of *TV Guide* magazine and your Bible. It's easy to see how they're different, and you might want to talk about this, but in what ways are they similar? What is the purpose of each one?

3. What kinds of programs are described in *TV Guide*? What kinds of books are found in the Bible? Though diverse in origin and nature, the biblical books are said by scholars to present a unified view of reality. What is this, described by one theologian as "the strange world of the Bible"? Do you think that there is a television world view? Why or why not? If so, what is it? If not, are there many different world views? Describe some of them.

4. Turn on your set and watch whatever is on for ten minutes, or through the next commercial break. Yes, I said *through* the "important message"; for, as you will see, these are a significant part of television and thus of our discussions.

5. Ten minutes or so have passed, and your set is turned off. Was it hard or easy to turn off the program? Why or why not? Are you wishing now that the leader would relent and let you watch the rest of the program?

6. What kind of program were you watching? How many similar programs are there? Is there anything that makes this program outstanding, even unique? Would you miss it if the network were to drop it from their schedule? How popular a program is it?

7. Did the commercial breaks contribute or detract from your viewing experience? Were they as interesting as the program? Do you think that as much care and expense were put into producing the commercials as the program itself?

8. If your program was fictional: What were the characters like? What class of society were they from? How did they relate to one another? Were their motives believable? Was the situation credible, or was this an adult fairy tale?

9. If the program was a comedy: What kind of comedy—situational, stand-up, farcical, or something else? Did the humor grow out of the situation, or was it at the expense of someone? Was it believable?

10. If the program was other than the above: What did the show say about life; that is, what seemed to be its underly-

ing values? How did it portray humanity?

11. What is your favorite television program? Why?

12. If you have enough people, divide into seven teams. Each team should take a different day of the week and examine that day's listings in *TV Guide* magazine. If you don't have enough people, let some teams examine two days' listings. What kinds of programs are on in the various time blocks? Is there any "religious" programming offered? When? What kind? Can you discover any secular programs that deal with religious or ethical values? Share your findings with the rest of the group.

13. What should be the purpose of television, its reason for being? Does this fit in with the Christian's mission of proclaiming the gospel? Could it? How? Do you see this happening? How and where?

14. Take a sheet of paper and divide it into seven sections, one for each day of the week. List the programs you usually view. How does your actual viewing match up with your statement of what you think the purpose of television is? How many hours do you watch TV in a typical week?

"And Now a Word from . . ."

O.K., you've spent about an hour together, exploring the tube and a little of what it brings into our homes. You have gained and shared a few insights into the world of television and into yourself. Now you can decide whether you want to plunge further into this confusing and fascinating world, or to sit back and allow the tube to mesmerize you. Either way has risks. On the one hand, you can regard television as just entertainment, and submit to its hypnotic effect, even to the point of being "squeezed into the world's mold." Or you can begin to look at this medium through the tinted spectacles of the gospel. At first, this might spoil a little of the entertainment, but in the long run it will make televiewing even more fun. And when you do want to watch a program for the sheer fun or escape it offers, you will know what you are doing. And you need not feel the need to apologize for it; the God who created the duckbill platypus surely understands our need to escape serious concerns for a spell.

This study is undertaken from the perspective of faith that expects the God of Israel to be popping up in all sorts of places, tempting and prodding his pilgrim people to rise up and follow him. The God who bypassed the high and mighty to choose a scraggly band of

slaves in Egypt; who appeared to Moses in thunder, fire, and cloud, but who spoke to Elijah like a still, small voice; and who dropped into our world as a baby coming inconveniently during a hard journey with no proper roof over his head—this same God just might speak to us again through what some disdainfully call the boob tube. "Can anything good come out of Nazareth?" is now "Can anything good come out of CBS?" Yes, it can, and if this book helps the church to see this, to separate the wheat from the chaff, and to celebrate this, it will have achieved its purpose.

"And Now a Word from . . ."

Welcome, friends, to "Life Can Be Rotten," where we will see just how desperate and hopeless life can be. Here we will ask the questions, Can a young woman fresh from the farm and mother's milk find happiness in the concrete canyons of the big city? Are all your neighbors' husbands seeing other women, thereby proving the thesis that men are no damn good? And of course, Which vixen threatens the happy home of Trudy Truluv—and will her nefarious schemes succeed? Also, in the course of a single day—Who will be committing suicide? Whose daughter will become pregnant? What bizarre surgery will be performed on which character? And, Will the operation be interrupted by a power shortage caused by an earthquake, a hurricane, a revolutionary's bomb, or by a plane left over from *Airport 1975* crashing into the hospital? In short, let's look at the programs that help you cope with typical, everyday problems to prove that "life can be rotten."

For the Leader

1. If you are meeting in the evening, arrange to have someone tape the audio portion of several soap operas. (If you have access to a video

WSAD: Channel 2

"LIFE CAN BE ROTTEN"

tape recorder, by all means use this.) Making an audio tape is a simple procedure that anyone can do with a small cassette recorder. Caution the person not to place the microphone too close to the TV set to avoid the high frequency whistling sound that so often is picked up when recording from television.

2. Have on hand: Several *TV Guide*s, Bibles, pencils/pens, note paper, and newsprint. For the "Further Probes" session, you will need: old magazines, including *True Romance* types, a slide projector, a reel-to-reel tape recorder, a tape splicing kit, and Simon and Garfunkel's "The Sounds of Silence."

3. Don't forget to pretape the "And Now a Word from ..." portions of this chapter. These can be enhanced by a melodramatic tone of voice. For another authentic touch, play a record of sentimental organ music in the background while you are reading. A little experimentation will show you how loud or soft it should be.

Such extras will add to the fun of your session. Use your imagination to create the best possible physical setting. For example, see if you can buy or borrow some reproductions of old movie posters advertising love and romance films. Or create your own posters based on current soap operas. Find some super-mushy love songs, old or new, and play them as the group is gathering.

For the Group

1. Turn on your TV set and watch a soap opera if you are meeting in the daytime. Or, listen to a tape of a soap opera, portions of several, or watch the video tape.

2. Go around the group and see if anyone has watched a soap opera lately. Are there any regular viewers? Describe current stories and characters. If the members are old enough, see how many radio soap operas they can remember, describing them in as much detail as possible. How were these different from current ones on TV?

3. Look through the *TV Guide*s. How many such programs are there? What portion of daytime telecasting do they represent? What other programs are offered at this time? Any similarities?

4. What makes a soap opera different from other forms of drama? Describe in as much detail as possible several of the heroes/heroines and villains in a current series. What seems to make them tick? Use your imagination and fill in the following for each one:

WSAD: Channel 2
"LIFE CAN BE ROTTEN"

_____'s favorite hobby/pastime would
(Name of Character)
probably be _____. _____'s
favorite song would probably be _____.
_____'s childhood was probably
_____. If _____ lived
next door, we would probably talk the most about
_____. If I could have just five minutes
with _____, I would want to tell him/her
_____.

Some would say that "Marcus Welby" is more soap opera than medical drama. Do you see any soap opera traits in this or other evening series?

"And Now a Word from . . ."

By now you should be getting into the substance of "Life Can Be Rotten." You are beginning to see into the inner workings of the soap opera, a place with its own set of people, conflicts, and values. Taken together these make up the world view of the soap opera. The writers, actors, and producers, of course, do not consciously promote anything as pretentious sounding as a world view, but it's there. And the audience, also unaware, is absorbing it and tacitly agreeing to it by continuing to watch such shows. They might have quite different views in everyday life, but by tuning in so as not to miss the next thrilling episode they consent to the program's views, values, and solutions to "life's pressing problems." Still another world view is presented in the Christian gospel. So now let's get on to the next thrilling discussion of "Life Can Be Rotten" to see how the two compare.

5. How does God fit into the world view of the soap opera? That is, what do you believe the following think of God: The hero/heroine? The bad guys/gals? Supporting characters? The writer and producers?

Describe what you think might be the major characteristics of their view of God.

6. What values seem to underlie the soap opera? If enough people are familiar with the different series, compare them. Are there any basic differences in emphasis or viewpoint? Another way of getting at this: take a look at the soap opera characters by filling in the following:

WSAD: Channel 2

"LIFE CAN BE ROTTEN"

a. _____ of _____ would say
   (character)   (program)

   that his/her purpose here on earth is _____.

b. _____ of _____ would

   say that the most important thing in life is

   _____. He/she shows that he/she means

   it by _____.
         (specific example)

7. The word "love" is frequently used in such stories. Discuss the ways the various characters use it. (Let us count the ways?) What are some possible definitions? How is the word used in the Scriptures? A theological handbook or wordbook, of which there are many, would be a helpful reference resource at this point.

"And Now a Word from . . ."
Both the Bible and the soap opera show people loving and hating, healing and killing, laughing and crying. There is a fundamental difference, however, in that the Bible portrays not just a series of interesting events about good and bad people—it shows the lives of men and women within the context of a world created by a God who acts upon and within their lives. The Bible shows how they react when confronted with this God, and it also seeks to draw us into such an encounter. Your group needs to probe what it is that the soap opera seeks to confront us with. Life *can* be rotten, as many episodes in the Bible amply demonstrate. (Think of all of Job's problems!) But what else can it be? And does our television viewing confront us with the other side of such questions, or does it appeal to the sadist, masochist, and voyeur within us?

8. If your group is large (over six or eight members), divide into units of three or four. Let each unit choose a different character from the list. Take a sheet of paper or newsprint, pens, and pencils, and divide the sheet into halves. Label one "Good Qualities" and the other "Hangups," or some such label. List all the good and bad characteristics for:

a. Adam   Genesis 2–3
b. Eve   Genesis 2–3
c. Abraham   Genesis 12–15
d. Sarah   Genesis 16–21
e. Jacob   Genesis 25:19–33
f. Moses   Exodus 2–6

WSAD: Channel 2
"LIFE CAN BE ROTTEN"

g. King Saul   I Samuel 9–13, 18–19
h. David   I Samuel 17–24; II Samuel 6–7; 9; 11–12
i. Job   Job 1–3
j. Ruth   Ruth
k. Peter   Matthew 4:18-22; 16:13-23; 17:1-8; 26:30-37;
               26:69-75; John 13:1-9; Acts 2-4
l. Paul   Galatians 1–2; Acts 8:1-8; 9; 14–16

For complete references to the above, check a concordance. Each group should select one person to record its findings and to report to the larger group. Allow about fifteen minutes for this. (If the entire group is no more than five or six, each person can select his/her own character.)

9. Did you find that the biblical authors cover up the bad qualities or overrate the good ones of the above? Discuss this in comparison to melodrama.

10. Now divide the group into pairs. Read Romans 7 and 8. What might Paul say to soap opera folk? Let one person take the role of Paul, the other a soap opera character. Interact as if Paul had met the person for counseling.

Further Probes

1. Divide into small groups—two to six in each group. Work out a skit based on one of the following biblical stories or characters; this should be in the form of a soap opera episode. If you find it difficult to get started, look over "The Loves of David" near the end of this section. This is presented as an example and should not be allowed to inhibit your own imagination. Create your own production based on:

a. Adam and Eve
b. Ruth and Boaz
c. Hosea and Gomer
d. Jonah
e. Parable: the prodigal son
f. John the Baptist, Salome, and Herod

If none of the above spark your imagination, select your own—the Bible is full of easily adaptable stories, as Hollywood discovered years ago.

Add characters, update the time or situation, but stick to the main plot or theme of the original. For extra fun, include background organ music and some ads from your sponsor.

After performing the skit, present some questions for discussion: What had to be changed in the original story to make it fit the mold of the soap opera? What had to be added or left out?

2. Bring out your old

WSAD: Channel 2
"LIFE CAN BE ROTTEN"

magazines, including some copies of the *True Romance* type, paste, scissors, poster paints, magic markers, and large sheets of cardboard.

Make one or more collages to show the contrast between love and humanity as seen in the soap opera and in the Old and New Testaments.

3. Ask someone ahead of time to tape as many episodes of different soap operas as possible. Pick out some of the highlights from each and dub them onto a single reel of tape. Rearrange the order. If you have some sound-effects records and top-forty albums, create an audio collage. Make it as funny as you can. Add your own commentary to create a new soap opera.

4. Use the above tape as part of the sound track for a slide or multimedia show. This could be just the right touch for a family fun night at the church. Shoot pictures of your group in the old stylized romantic scenes. You can also take slide pictures from TV soap operas; turn your set to bright and high contrast, set your camera shutter speed at 1/60 a second and load it with high-speed slide film. Take pictures of the "romance" magazines also. Combine these with slides that you make from slick-paper magazines via the lift-off pro-

cess, and you will have an intriguing media mix. An additional possibility is to add scenes from a romantic Hollywood movie. Many of these, including relatively recent ones, such as *Love Story*, are available in 8, Super 8, and 16mm format. Show the film in between your slides, and you'll have an unforgettable presentation.

"The Loves of David" Selected excerpts

Our first scene comes from an episode well into the series. We have seen David, emerging from nowhere, rise to the top of the Jehovah Mineral Corporation. He had taken on Jehovah's toughest competitor, the goliath Philistine 66 Fuel Consortium, and bested them in a fight-to-the-finish competition for oil and mineral rights in Outer Mongolia. Taken into the firm by Saul Farrel as a junior partner, he has endured Saul's insane jealousy and has survived Saul's maneuvering to remove him from the corporation board, a proxy fight out of which David has finally emerged as the new president. He had a series of disappointments in love before finally meeting Michelle and beginning their subsequent seventy-seven-episode courtship and engagement. Their

"The Loves of David"

The Torrid Love Affair That Threatened an Empire

**1:30 P.M.
WSAD CHANNEL 2**

EVERY WEEKDAY

wedding was a lavish affair, to which almost all of daytime America, tissues in hand, were witnesses. Only, of course, David and Michelle have not lived happily ever after, for this is a soap opera, not a fairy tale. So now we encounter David on a hot summer evening in his Manhatten penthouse apartment.

David: It's so quiet with Michelle gone. We shouldn't have quarreled so violently. What was it about, anyway? It's too bad we just can't seem to make it together anymore. God knows we've tried. We were so blissful those first few years. I wonder what went wrong. Is it my job, the overwhelming task of running the largest energy corporation in the world? It's so demanding, so awesome to know that the homes and businesses of millions of people depend upon my making the right decisions, in maintaining a ceaseless flow of energy . . .

It's so hot and stuffy in here this evening, even with the air conditioning on. I think I'll stroll out onto the terrace to watch the sun set over Jersey. *(He opens the sliding door and walks over to the terrace railing. The city lights are just beginning to come on. The music begins to swell.)*

WSAD: Channel 2
"LIFE CAN BE ROTTEN"

Ah ... this is better. Still warm, but there's a good breeze up here. The setting sun casts such a lovely glow over the other buildings. Hmmm, what's that over there? *(He looks intently across to a nearby roof top. The camera follows his gaze, and we see, a few stories below, a bikini-clad woman reading by a pool.)*

Now that's all right. It would certainly be interesting to meet her ... but no, I shouldn't ... and yet, why not? Michelle is away for the weekend. I've been working so hard lately. I need some rest, someone to talk to who won't nag the way Michelle does. But what if she doesn't want to meet me? Assuming that I can find out who she is ... but of course I can find out. I can send Reeves over to check with the doorman of her building. A twenty-dollar bill will do the trick. And when she finds out who I am—of course she will want to meet me. Yes, that's what I'll do. Reeves! Reeves! Come here. I have a job for you. *(The music, now a tremulo, has swelled to a crescendo as David turns to go back into his living room.)*

Narrator: What will come of David's impulsive resolve to meet the unknown beauty in the building across the street? What long-suppressed passions and forbidden desires lie coiled in his manly body, waiting to be unleashed? Who is this tantalizing beauty—and *whose* is she? Will David risk his financial kingdom for love? And what about Michelle? Be sure to stay tuned tomorrow, and every day, for each exciting episode of "The Loves of David"!

(A hundred or so episodes later)

Narrator: For the sake of his love for the beautiful Sheba, David, head of the world-straddling Jehovah Mineral Corporation, has risked his reputation and corporate presidency. David's wife, Michelle, has left him. Sheba is married to Eugene Hittites, a division manager in David's company. To the lovers' consternation, Sheba has just discovered that she is pregnant with David's child. We join the star-crossed lovers at their favorite hideaway restaurant where, in our last episode, Sheba has just broken the news of her pregnancy to David.

Sheba: David—David, speak to me, darling. Don't you understand what I've just told you?

David: *(Visibly taken aback)*

Yes, dear, I do. I am just trying to assimilate the impact.

Sheba: *(Near tears)* Oh, David, David, David. I am so sorry to tell you this way. In my woman's dreams about us I yearned to have a child by you. But not like this, no, not like this at all!

David: Yes, Sheba, dear one. I longed to have a child by you. Michelle would never hear of it—she was so worried about losing her figure. But not like this. This could ruin us both.

Sheba: Then what can we do, David?

David: You are absolutely sure about this? But of course you are; I can see that in your eyes. Well then, are you certain that the child is mine? Couldn't it be Eugene's? After all, he was home for a few days between field trips last month.

Sheba: Oh, David, of course I am certain. He has been working so hard for the corporation, preparing those endless reports and traveling around the world. Even when he was home, he worked far into the night. And besides, since being with you I don't think I could stand for him to touch me . . .

David: But you must. Yes, that's it! I'll have him called

home. I'll say that I need him for a special project that only he can handle. There's still time. Sheba, you must go to him then.

Sheba: Oh, David, no—it just wouldn't be right! It would seem that I was untrue to you.

David: I know, dear, but it's a sacrifice both of us must make. I'm sorry that you especially must bear the brunt of it, but you must for the sake of our love. You know that neither of us can go through a divorce just at this time.

Sheba: But what if it doesn't work? You don't know Eugene, David. He's so wrapped up in his work. When he's on a project, he scarcely stops to eat or rest. Or to even talk with me, let alone sleep with me.

David: If this doesn't work, then we'll have to resort to more drastic measures.

Sheba: Drastic measures? You mean . . . ?

David: Yes, Sheba, I do.

Sheba: No, David, no, no, *no!* I could never abort your child. Not only that, but it's against my religion.

David: Against your *religion?!*

Sheba: Oh yes, darling. I know, I don't seem like a very religious person. I haven't been inside a church since my wedding, but I do believe, deep down, and I believe it would be wrong to take away the life of our child. It would ruin everything that is right and beautiful between us.

David: Then you must entice Eugene to come to you, Sheba, you must.

(Silence for a moment, as David reaches across the table to hold her hand. The camera slowly zooms in on Sheba's quivering lips as she whispers haltingly.)

Sheba: Y-Yes, David . . . I know . . . I-I'll try. I really will. But you must know—my heart will not be in it. And if our plan doesn't work, what then? *(The camera closes in on their clasped, trembling hands. Fade out as the organ music swells up.)*

Narrator: Friends, what then? Will Sheba succeed in her subterfuge? Will Eugene find out their forbidden secret? If so, will the resulting scandal destroy David's career? Can a man who selflessly has given so much find happiness for himself when the woman whom he truly loves is the wife of another man? Stay tuned tomorrow—and every weekday—for more thrilling chapters of "The Loves of David." And now this important message from those wonderful people who create daytime drama.

Announcer: "As the World Turns" toward "The Edge of Night," we have but "One Life to Live," and so the question remains whether "The Doctors" at "General Hospital," engaged in the constant "Search for Tomorrow," can find "The Guiding Light" to teach them "How to Survive a Marriage" and create "For All My Children" "Another World" better than this. Or, will "The Secret Storm" overwhelm them?

"And Now a Word from . . ."

The story of King David is presented in the Bible with few frills. He is pictured as chosen by God, through the prophet Samuel, to be king. His strong leadership and magnanimous qualities are seen in many episodes. But his passion leads him into deep trouble, in the infamous affair with Bathsheba and later with his sons. There is no cover-up or apology for his adultery. David is wrong, and the prophet Nathan tells him this to his face. Today, such a lapse might be justified, even lauded. How might the melodramatist attempt this? Can you see any attempt to do so in "The Loves of David"? As a project, you might want to write some further episodes of the series. What plan might David come up with to remove Eugene from the picture? Or can you think of a *deus ex machina* to get the lovers off the hook and thus keep David "pure" from bloodguiltiness?

Some Worship Suggestions

A hallmark of Christian gatherings is the praise of God and the celebration of his grace. This can be true when gathering to probe the impact of the various forms of television, even soap operas. The following are suggestions only, given to start your ideas flowing. Such worship works

WSAD: Channel 2
"LIFE CAN BE ROTTEN"

best when it is a group-designed celebration. The traditional order or structure, however, is followed because even contemporary worship needs a skeleton, and the church has learned through the ages that regardless of outward form, the old pattern discerned in the sixth chapter of Isaiah is a good one. If you are meeting in a home with very limited time, you will want to use only one or two of the suggestions, which should provide a fitting means of closing the sessions. The more elaborate suggestions should be useful at a retreat or conference setting.

I. "The Edge of Night"
   A. Prelude: The room should be in near darkness. Play Simon and Garfunkel's "The Sounds of Silence."
   B. True Confessions: Have several people read, in rapid succession, some lines of spite and vengeance from real or imaginary soap operas. Or play your audio collage, or show your slide/media show based on soap operas.
   C. Reading: Genesis 3
II. "As The World Turns"
   A. Repentance: Make a brief statement about *metanoia*, repentance, and the turning around of the mind and heart. You could paraphrase parts of Isaiah 40 in such a statement.
   B. The Assurance of Pardon: Isaiah 9:2 and John 3:16
   C. Act of Praise: A hymn or dance
III. "The Guiding Light"
   A. Reading: Selections from John 1
   B. Meditation: Share some thoughts or comments Christ might make to current soap opera characters.
      Do a readers' theater version of one of the episodes your

WSAD: Channel 2

"LIFE CAN BE ROTTEN"

group has created, or "The Loves of David." Respond to the situation as Christ might (and don't forget, the Lord has a good sense of humor, too).

IV. "The Search for Tomorrow"
   A. Prayer: Share concerns.
   B. Song: "Day by Day" from *Godspell*
   C. Benediction: Pass the Peace around the group.

KZAP: Channel 3–

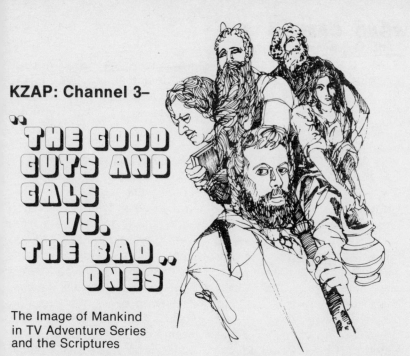

"THE GOOD GUYS AND GALS VS. THE BAD ONES"

The Image of Mankind
in TV Adventure Series
and the Scriptures

"And Now A Word from . . ."

Captain Marvelous America, his red, white, and blue cape swirling behind him, swoops down on the band of criminals . . . . Former Detective Chief Ironguts, his jet-propelled wheelchair crashing through the door, surprises the Ratsy Gang as they are about to torture his secretary . . . . Lotus McBantellichi, the Black-Polish-Italian-Chinese-American female detective, her rumpled trench coat buttoned up to ward off the cold night air, steps out of the shadows as a sinister figure approaches . . . . After climbing up the cable in the elevator shaft, while dodging a barrage of bullets, Bat Helmut follows his prey out through the skylight to the rooftop. There, ninety-seven stories above the busy city streets, he grapples with his arch foe . . . . Marshall Martial stands in the middle of the dusty street, his right hand poised above his pearl-handled gun with its seventy-six notches . . . .

For the Leader

1. Arrange to watch all or portions of an adventure show which is a part of a continuing series. Chances are that there will be several no matter what night you meet.

2. Have on hand: TV set, a roll of wrapping paper or a newsprint pad, felt-tipped pens, *TV Guide,* copies of this

KZAP: Channel 3
"THE GOOD VS. THE BAD"

book, a stack of adventure magazines, pencils and paper, Bibles, and your cassette recorder with a recording of the "And Now a Word from . . ." segments.

For the Group

1. Does the collage of adventure heroes (for *hero* read "hero or heroine" throughout) sound familiar? Make a list of the adventure programs you watch. Mark them "Occasionally," "Frequently," and "Won't Miss." Compare your list with others in the group.

2. Turn on your TV set and watch part or all of an adventure program, depending on how much time you have. How does the show open? Does it immediately capture your interest? What crises arise during the episode? (If you really want to get analytical, ask someone to count or time them to see how frequently they arise.) How does our hero meet and solve them?

Where would you say the emphasis of the show lies: action, violence, gadgetry, surprise elements, characterization, or something else?

How do the camera-work and editing contribute to this? Also notice the pacing of the story and of commercial breaks.

3. Divide into fours. Each four is to pick a well-known adventure series. Through words and action give clues to the other groups so that they can guess what show you are presenting.

"And Now a Word from . . ."

By now you have exchanged some facts and feelings about one popular type of television fare. The form may vary from year to year. One season, cop shows are big. Then a network comes up with a war series that's a hit in the ratings game, and soon every new program has a similar setting. The Westerns, like the swallows of Capistrano, make their cyclical return to preeminence. There seems to be a restless spirit within most of us that craves excitement, even if it must be found vicariously in front of a twenty-one-inch screen. As old as humanity, this spirit might have been the cause of Adam and Eve's first tasting the forbidden fruit. As we read on through the Bible we see a number of exciting episodes, proving that adventure is not just a part of secular humanity, but suggesting, indeed, that the greatest adventure of all might be the real-life search of God for his people, and for you in particular.

4. Let each group of four choose a popular adventure hero. Each group should have a seven-foot length of wrap-

ping paper or newsprint and several felt-tipped pens. Spread the paper on the floor and have someone lie on the paper while the others trace the outline of his body. This outlined figure represents your chosen hero. Divide the body into head, torso, arms, and legs. Each person chooses one part and beside it on the paper jots down everything he or she can imagine about it—the type/texture of skin, the smell, the clothing, any special characteristics. The "head man" should also attempt to describe what goes on inside the head. How does the character feel about himself, others? Does he believe in God—or what?

Work at this for no more than four minutes, then share with the other members of your "body committee" what you have written. Do all the parts fit together, or do you need to work out a compromise? Let each group share its descriptions.

5 In the same quartets choose a Bible story and create a short skit based on it as if it were an episode from a current TV adventure series. Some possible stories are Sampson and Delilah, David and Goliath, Jonah, or episodes from Paul's life as recorded in Acts. Spend no more than ten minutes prepar-ing this (don't worry about dramatic perfection), and then share it with the others.

What elements had to be changed to make the original story suitable for TV?

6. Some police/detective shows depict both sides quickly resorting to violence. What are the differences between the two sides? How do the police and the hero treat the criminal once he's apprehended (assuming that they didn't treat him to a spectacular death)? Does the hero ever give you the impression that the ends justify the means? Does he or she ever seem to have moments of self-doubt or regret? Is he or she *always* successful?

7. Look up some of the following characters in the Bible. These are often described as heroes, but do the Scriptures reveal more than the hero stereotype?

Abraham—Genesis 12–18
Rahab—Joshua 2:1–21
Jacob—Genesis 25–33
Deborah—Judges 5:2–31
Sampson—Judges 13–16
Judith—See the book
David—I & II Samuel
Jael—Judges 5:2–31
Jonah—See the book
Priscilla—Romans 16:3–4
Peter—Luke 5. Matthew 14:22–33; 17:1–8; 26. John 13

KZAP: Channel 3

"THE GOOD VS. THE BAD"

8. Think of a TV villain. In your small group do your impression of him by acting or pantomine for the others.

What kind of person is he or she? How is he or she portrayed in the series? Is there an established pattern, or are the villains different from one another? What motivates him or her? Is the conflict physical, intellectual, or spiritual? Is it possible to see the villain as a child of God, or are the viewers' feelings manipulated so that they can only hate him or her?

How much influence do you think the TV stereotypes have on us? Do the characters provide us with models to emulate? Do the villains affect our views of crime and punishment, of law and order?

9. Do you see any change or growth in the TV hero? Has he or she changed a view or habit at the end of an adventure? Or is there a change in the way he or she relates to someone? The Scriptures speak a great deal about growth and change in such passages as John 3:1-21 and II Corinthians 5:14-21.

10. Close this session by returning to your group of four, reading the Bible passages, and making a character chart.

Character Chart

Divide your sheet of paper in fourths and fill in:

TV Hero
(Your Choice)
Things I like about him/her:

Biblical Character
(Your Choice)
I like about him/her:

Things I don't like:

I don't like:

Me-Today
What I like about me:

Me-Tomorrow
Things about me I hope to change:

What I don't like:

Here's how I plan to make the change:

Each person should spend three or four minutes on this. Then share with the other three in the group. Close with a sentence prayer, each group leaving silently so as not to disturb the others who might not be finished.

Further Probes

1. Let the group members leaf through a stack of adventure magazines and comics. Describe the heroes in them. How similar are they to the TV characters you've talked about?

2. Gunfight at the I'm O.K.—You're Not O.K. Corral. Ever since 1948 when the shrewd actor-businessman William Boyd sold his Hopalong Cassidy films to

television, the Western has been an important part of the TV adventure scene. As with all formula drama, it has many conventions such as:

The hero—rootless, drifting across the West.

The rescue.

The street fight, with the inevitable dunkings in the horse trough.

The tavern brawl—with many comic aspects.

One or more gun duels.

The chase (posse, band of Indians, etc.).

The climatic fight or gun battle.

Can you think of other conventions or variations of the above?

Divide into groups of four and work out a skit using

KZAP: Channel 3
"THE GOOD VS. THE BAD"

conventions from the Western. Base your plot on a story from the Bible.

"And Now a Word from ..."

Frequently the Western seems to be based on the premise that only the hero is O.K., to use a term from transactional analysis. Not only is the villain not O.K., but seldom is anyone else either. The townspeople are usually cowardly or indifferent. The sidekick is too funny or bumbling to be of real help. The heroine is pretty, but weak or dumb. Only the hero has the right combination of raw courage, competence, physical strength, and skill to save the day. It's a win or lose world with no room for compromise or negotiation. This is a good formula for fantasy, but in real life if I am the only one who is O.K., the consequences can be as disastrous as any shoot-out.

3. Some other types of adventure programs worth exploring further:

a. The Hero as Crime Fighter:
   What are the conventions of this genre? What needs do such shows fulfill, especially in an era of rising crime? What view of

Batman and Robin

KZAP CHANNEL 3
4:30 P.M.

with a host of guest villains

human nature do such shows present?

b. Woman as Hero:
   A new trend is developing—women are beginning to emerge not as partners who must rely on a man, but as tough, capable heroes in their own right. Describe the women heading up such programs. What combination of traditional "masculine" and "feminine" traits make up their character?

4. Television Spoofs:
   Some variety-comedy shows such as "The Carol Burnett Show" frequently present

good sketches satirizing some of the silly aspects of television, including the adventure heroes. Can anyone in the group recall any of these?

Check your *TV Guide* magazine to see if "Batman" is being rerun in your area. It is often shown in "kiddy time" in the late afternoon or early evening, but it wasn't just kids who made the show an instant hit when it appeared in 1966. Adam West as the Caped Crusader was either hilariously funny or tremendously fantastic, depending on the age of the viewer. My young children wondered why my wife and I were always laughing at the height of some exciting rescue or flight. Watch several episodes and list the clichés of adventure stories which it parodies.

Note the McGuffey Reader style of moralisms, such as: Robin is thrown, or falls from a building. He cries out to Batman for help. Our hero hurls his Batrope at his falling assistant. Robin catches it in his teeth (his hands are tied behind his back!) and is pulled to safety. He thanks Batman, not only for rescuing him but also for making him brush his teeth all those years. The masked hero responds with, "Yes, Robin, it shows the importance of good dental hygiene!" All this with a straight face.

KZAP: Channel 3
"THE GOOD VS. THE BAD"

There are dozens of such delightful moments in this series with super-heroes and equally delightful super-villains. Is such humor a healthy sign? What does it do to the mythology of the hero?

5. Divide into small groups and ask each one to come up with a skit in which a super-Christian (choose your own name or title) saves the day. The following is an example to get you started thinking.

"Faster than a speedy prayer! Able to leap tall church spires in a single bound! More powerful than the Gospel Train! Look, up in the sky! It's a bird! It's a plane! It's Super Saint!

"Welcome, friends, to the adventures of Super Saint, the program that proves that your strength will be as the strength of ten when your heart is pure. We last left Super Saint hot on the trail of Dr. Satana, the mad fiend who was sneaking into church offices and sticking tar into the workings of the mimeograph machines, thereby bringing the work of the church to a halt. Paralyzed without their mimeographed reports and unable to worship without Sunday bulletins, the church leaders of Gotham had called in Super Saint to track down the fiendish master criminal."

If your time is limited, let

KZAP: Channel 3

"THE GOOD VS. THE BAD"

each group write just the opening of the program. The above seems far-fetched, but have you seen the comic books with such heroes winning the day for God?

6. Over the centuries the church has designated some of its adventurers as saints. What is the popular view of a saint? Of a sinner? Look through I Corinthians; note that Paul addresses them as "called to be saints" despite all their unsaintly problems. Divide into small groups again and study one of the following passages:

Romans 6–7
Galatians 5–6:10
Ephesians 4–5:20
Philippians 2:1–18; 3:7–21
Colossians 3:1–17

Do you have any additional insights into the meaning of saint or sinner? Share your observations with the entire group. If you want to pursue this topic further, have someone read and report on the two novels by Graham Greene, which deal with the issue of sainthood, *The Power and the Glory* and *End of the Affair*. Mr. Greene presents us with two very unheroic or unsaintly saints.

If we are called to be "sinning saints," how does this compare with the view of man's nature as depicted in your favorite TV adventure yarn?

7. Some members of the group might want to read through the book of Acts as raw material for a TV series. How would you approach the book? Choose a name for the series and write an outline or scenario for some of the programs.

An Extended Time Activity

This activity is designed for a retreat or special project. It will require some funds as well as time and patience, but the results can be worth it. You can buy excerpts from famous adventure movies—Westerns, war, detective, and even "Batman"—for a few dollars in Super or Regular 8mm film. These will run from about three dollars for a four-minute black and white reel to seven or eight dollars for a twelve-minute reel. Buy several different titles, an extra reel, and splicing tape. Anyone who takes many home movies will probably have a movie editor, splicer, and the know-how to show you how to cut and splice your films together. If you have a movie camera, you can add to the fun by shooting scenes acted out by members of your group. You can create your own titles and captions. Buy a roll of 160 Ektachrome movie film, and you can even shoot short scenes from your favorite TV series; there will be a slight roll effect in the finished film, but this won't be too bad since you'll be using short scenes. To get your imagination going, here's a possible scenario:

The Beatitudes According to Super-Heroes

Video	Audio (This can be read live or put on a tape.)
Scene of your group. A wild party or tavern brawl.	"Blessed are the poor in spirit . . . for theirs is the kingdom of heaven.
The aftermath of a shoot-out, the heroine in distress or faces of your group crying in exaggerated manner.	Blessed are those who mourn . . .
Enter the Super-Hero. Shots of the "little people" in your films; or your group pantomining "who me?" or other such "meek" acts.	for they shall be comforted. Blessed are the meek . . .
Shots of wild celebration, or of a desert—good pollution shots might be funny.	for they shall inherit the earth.
Some Westerns have episodes of the hero staggering through a desert (or you could stage your own); or shots of the villains taking advantage of the little people; or for a touch of irony use any scenes of Indians your Western might have.	Blessed are those who hunger and thirst for righteousness . . .
A shot of a celebration or party; happy faces.	for they shall be satisfied.
Our villain pleading for mercy;	Blessed are the merciful . . .

KZAP: Channel 3
"THE GOOD VS. THE BAD"

a lynch mob; a shoot-'em-up scene; our hero pounding away at the villain.

Close-up of our hero/heroine. If you used your own members for this, have him give her an oversized valentine or a heart-shaped box of candy.

for they shall obtain mercy.

Shots of them looking off into the distance; a nature scene; a church; or you can buy excerpts from DeMille's *The Ten Commandments*.

Blessed are the pure in heart for they shall see God.

Use part of a war movie here; a gun duel; couple arguing; bar-room brawl; etc.

Blessed are the peace-makers . . .

More close-ups of our hero, preferrably battered after a fight.

for they shall be called sons of God.

Villain (s) doing horrible deeds to the little people.

Blessed are those who are persecuted for righteousness' sake . . .

The Big Rescue.

for theirs is the kingdom of heaven.

More scenes of villains and oppression.

Blessed are you when men revile you and persecute you.

A shot of a celebration; the last scenes from many films would work.

Rejoice and be glad, for your reward is great in heaven.''

KZAP: Channel 3
"THE GOOD VS. THE BAD"

The above is designed for laughs. If you want a more serious film collage, suitable for worship as well as family fun nights, you could make one up from the fine newsreels that Castle Films has produced and made available. These include the highlights of every year from 1937 in Regular 8mm format and from the early 1960s in Super 8mm. Among them are moving scenes of our national triumphs and tragedies, so I am certain that you can find more than enough material in three or four of these 150-foot reels of films (about twelve minutes). If your local photography store doesn't carry these films, you will find the address of Castle Films in the bibliography and resources section of this book.

Your completed film collage should be from three to five minutes in length, depending on how much film footage you choose. Remember, it's usually better to use too little than too much so that your audio isn't strung out too long. The narrator can read the text as the film unfolds, or you could combine the reading with music and put both on tape. This latter is more difficult, requiring careful planning. You will need to match the sound and pictures and then make sure that both the projector and the tape player are started at the same point each time. Either way you will have an engrossing visual interpretation.

An Adventure in Worship: A Celebration Based on the Prodigal Son
  I. At Home
      Call to Worship
      Song: "Morning Has Broken" or "Happy the Man" by Sebastian Temple
      Reading of Creation Story: Genesis 1
          (Slides could be used with this. Have four readers for the Genesis passages: the narrator, Adam, Eve, and God.)
      Reading: Luke 15:11-12
 II. Going to a Far Country
      Reading: Genesis 3:1-8
      Song: "One Tin Soldier," the Beatles' "She's Leaving Home," or "500 Miles." Play a recording of one of these unless the group knows it well.
      Reading: Luke 15:13-16
      Act of Confession: Write a prayer using the imagery of the prodigal running away from home.

KZAP: Channel 3

"THE GOOD VS. THE BAD"

III. Coming to Ourselves

Reading: Genesis 3:9-19

Song: "Genesis One" by Carlton Young; or another song dealing with new beginnings.

Reading: Luke 15:17-19

IV. Returning to Our Father

Reading: Genesis 3:20-21

Song: Make it an exuberant one, such as "If I Had a Hammer."

Reading: Luke 15:20-24

V. Hearing the Word

Some Possibilities for the Meditation:

1. Compare the Genesis and prodigal son stories as examples of our desire to go it alone without God and searching for adventure in the wrong places. Play the song "My Way."

2. Base some remarks on the temptation of Christ in Matthew 4. The three temptations could be seen as three adventurous paths beckoning to him to go it alone, to do things his way rather than God's.

3. If some of your members tackled the film collage project, show this along with some interpretive comments tying it in with your worship theme.

4. Take a familiar TV program (or character) and use it as a take-off for some remarks on the way of the Cross as adventuresome living. (For example, a few years ago there were a number of sermons using "Mission Impossible.") The lives of the saints, from Paul to Martin Luther King, Jr., offer many illustrations.

VI. Sharing the Celebration

Pass around balloons to one another with the words of "Peace" or other such greeting. If practical, the group could sing a song and then go out from the church and give balloons to those whom they meet. (Our youth did this once as part of a retreat held in our church building. They received a number of interesting reactions from people going in and out of a dime store—quite an adventure.)

Song: "There's A Church Within Us," "Peace, My Friends," or "God Give Us Your Peace"

Benediction.

KZAP: Channel 3
"THE GOOD VS. THE BAD"

Further notes on the worship service: some of the songs can be sung by the entire group; others you might have sung by a soloist or small group, or played on a record or tape player.

An additional possibility for enriching the service is Francis Thompson's poem "The Hound of Heaven," which fits in well with the prodigal son theme. You could read all of it at some point (perhaps it could be the meditation) or divide it up, similar to the Genesis passages, and read portions of it at various points in the service.

PRO
PROMI

Television Advertising and Christian Values

MISES SES

WLIE: Channel 4—

"And Now a Word from..."

Friends, are you one of those who complain about television commercials? Do you walk out of the room for a sandwich or turn down the volume whenever a commercial comes on? Well, stop—look—and listen the next time! Where would television be without those wonderful men in white coats showing you with charts and clear glass stomachs which miracle medicine works the fastest? Would you bite the hand that feeds you such inspiring programs? Who would pay the bills? And how would you know which laxative or hair coloring to buy—for we all know how crammed with factual information those impor-tant messages are. So friends, stop complaining and give thanks to the unsung men and women who have made television what it is today. And remember, a series of inde-pendent laboratory tests proves conclusively that in most cases, nine out of ten people who watch TV com-mercials do.

For the Leader

1. The leader, or convener, should read each "And Now a Word from ..." for the group, or play the cassette recording of them, at the suggested places in the discussion/activity guide.

2. Have on hand: a TV set or an audio cassette recording of ads from television—or, of

WLIE: Channel 4
"PROMISES, PROMISES"

course, a video tape recording of a wide variety of ads taped during the course of the week. Also—paper, newsprint, pens or pencils, felt-tipped markers, old magazines, Simon and Garfunkel's album *Parsley, Sage, Rosemary and Thyme,* and a record player. Some useful additional resources are *Discovery in Advertising* by Richard Payne and Robert Heyer, a box of TV commercials (Check with the manager of your local television station. The commercials, on small rolls of 16mm film, are thrown out when a new ad series or campaign replaces the old. Some stations will give their old ones away to church leaders who explain that they want them for educational purposes while others will not.), a 16mm film splicer, and splicing tape.

For the Group

1. Turn on the television set and watch several ads. Don't worry if none are on at first—you won't have to wait long, unless you're tuned to the Public Broadcasting Station.

Or play your audio tape of ads recorded earlier.

Or play your video tape of spots (10-15 minutes).

2. List the products being advertised. What audiences are the ads beamed at? How do you think the advertiser views the audience? As warm, intelligent human beings? Or as childish Neanderthals? Get specific here—don't lump *all* admen together (5 minutes).

3. What basic human needs do the ads promise to meet? The following idea is to get you started thinking: Starkist features Charlie the Tuna who's always trying to measure up to Starkist's standards, but never quite makes it. All of us share with Charlie this need to be accepted, and thus we dread being told "Sorry, Charlie." For even deeper probing—what does the gospel's claim of the grace of God have to say to the Charlies of this world? (10 minutes).

4. What does the ad producer use to catch and hold your attention? A general checklist includes color, music, humor, style of editing and photography matched to the product, unusual camera shots, beautiful people and famous stars and authority figures, colorful scenery, drama, cartoon format, and louder than usual sound (5 minutes).

5. Divide into groups of four. Your group has just one minute to choose a product advertised on TV and two minutes to work out a charade describing it. As each group presents theirs (keep this to two or three minutes a group),

the others try to guess the product (10-15 minutes).

6. Do you use any of the products in the ads discussed so far? Why or why not? Do you think that the ad campaign for the product influenced you? How? Imagine that you are in a store confronted with two different brands (I'm making it easy for you, since you actually might be face-to-face with ten or more) of the same kind of detergent, cereal, hair product, or toothpaste. How do you decide which brand to buy? List the various factors that might enter into such a decision (5-10 minutes).

7. How many of the products which you have seen advertised, at any time, are actually necessary to sustain life? To make this as graphic as possible, tape up a large sheet of newsprint. Divide the sheet into three sections. On the right list the products which are necessities, in the center list those which are important but not absolutely necessary, and on the left, those products which are frivolous. Choose the person whose birthday is nearest to April Fools' Day to be the scribe (and reporter if you divide into smaller groups) (10-15 minutes).

"And Now a Word from . . ."

Madison Avenue's steel and concrete towers are a long way

WLIE: Channel 4
"PROMISES, PROMISES"

from the mudbrick ziggurats of ancient Babylon, but the desires and motivations of human beings seem to remain about the same. Ancient Israel had not settled for "the real thing," the God of Abraham and Moses. Instead they had accepted a poor substitute, the gods and subhuman values of their pagan neighbors. Thus, as their prophets had warned, the Israelites lost their homes, their holy city of Jerusalem, and the temple. All who were not killed or run off as fugitives had been dragged away to a life of slavery in Babylon. There they endured the torments of their captors until, many years later, they learned that the God whom they had rejected was still with them and about to set them free. The captive prophet who wrote most of Isaiah 40–55 announced their coming freedom, but also issued a strong warning that they never again settle for "that which is not bread."

For the Group

8. Read Isaiah 55:1-3. List the promises made in the ads discussed so far. Write the ad and promise side by side. How does the advertiser state or imply that the product will deliver? Do you think that it can? Relate the second verse of the Isaiah passage to this.

WLIE: Channel 4
"PROMISES, PROMISES"

Go back and look at your list of necessary and frivolous products. Which are "not bread" or do not "satisfy"?

As an alternative to discussing the above stage a mock trial of one or more products. Choose a judge to preside, a prosecuting attorney to bring the charges against the product, a defense attorney to refute the charges, a jury (four to six persons), and a series of prosecution and defense witnesses. To involve more people, the attorneys may have one or more assistants. The judge presides, swears in witnesses, keeps order, clarifies questions, and gives instructions when necessary. The prosecutor states the charges—such as "I am going to prove to you that Brand _____ is not necessary; indeed, that it is a waste of our resources and money, and should therefore be banned from manufacture and advertising." After each witness is called, the defense has the right to cross-examine, as does the prosecutor when the defense witnesses are called. Such a trial will require preparation, and could easily take from forty-five to sixty minutes.

9. Read Isaiah 53, then list all the patent medicine ads you can recall. To what needs in the viewer do they appeal? How do the ads support or back up their claims? What is their view of human suffering? Compare this to Isaiah 53. How can an aspirin culture cope with the concept of a suffering servant, or the idea that suffering may have redemptive possibilities, and therefore at times may be voluntarily entered into? Try to recall the words of a headache or upset stomach medicine ad. Substitute the word "God" for the medicine, and any appropriate religious term for the malady and cure. Have you encountered such a brand of religion in actual life? How can such products encourage us to run away from the problems and frustrations of life? How can

"Speedy Al" Kaseltzer on the Dock

WLIE CHANNEL 4 8:00 P.M.

Was he secretly at the bottom of a nationwide heartburn ring?

our religion become a form of escapism?

10. Read Mark 8:34-37. Compare Jesus' command to deny ourselves and take up our cross with the invitations in the ads. Do any of the ads encourage us to face up to ourselves, to our temptations, weaknesses, and problems? What fantasies do they encourage or feed upon? Are these healthy? Do you see any tendency to promote an abdication of individual responsibility—for overeating, overdrinking, overspending, and overindulgence of the body?

"And Now a Word from . . ."

All of us live with our fantasies and dreams. These provide not only relief from present boredom and tension but also the inspiration for making "what ought to be" a reality. The Old Testament prophet Joel described the coming age of God's perfect reign as a time when "your old men shall dream dreams, and your young men shall see visions." The adman, following his own profit dream, is a keen student of the fantasies and dreams of others. Not only does he seek through such tools as motivational research to find out what they are but also to implant a few new ones. Once he discovers our desires or

WLIE: Channel 4
"PROMISES, PROMISES"

creates new wants, his job becomes one of convincing us that his brand can make that dream a reality. He is just as much in the business of selling *dreams* as products.

Further Probes

1. Write the following dreams or values on a sheet of newsprint and then tape it to a wall. Everyone should spend a minute or two looking the list over and thinking of products to go with the items. Then ask for volunteers (no more than a fourth of the total group) to represent each dream/value. Each volunteer should stand up and call off a dream/value, write it in large letters on a sheet of paper and pin it to his/her clothing. As the volunteers walk around the room the others in the group should join them when they think of a product which can fulfill the dream/value. After everyone has one or more partners, the group sits down and each "product" person discloses his/her product and how it will bring the dream into being. Some "dream" persons will have two or more "product" persons, but *all* should have at least *one* "product" partner.

For a variation of the above, make up your own products and brands—as far out as you please.

WLIE: Channel 4

"PROMISES, PROMISES"

Dreams/Values

Beauty/Attractiveness	Fame/Fortune	Love and Friendship
Social Acceptance	Success	Social Prestige
Romance/Sex	Fun/Pleasure	Health, Other?

2. Listen to and discuss Simon and Garfunkel's spoof song "The Big Bright Green Pleasure Machine" from their album *Parsley, Sage, Rosemary and Thyme.* What problems will the BBGPM solve? How? (The song could also be played at the beginning of your session as the members are arriving.)

3. For further probing of Isaiah 55, compare the prophet's warning with the following spot developed by the United Methodists:

"Maybe I'm just lonely. Maybe I just feel sorry for myself. I have a good home, a good husband. The kids seem to be making it—not that we seem to really know. It's all kind of blah. I-I feel like all my life I've been climbing up a ladder. Now I'm at the top, and there's nothing up there. I guess I feel like I've been cheated or something. I feel like I want to cry half the time, but I wouldn't even know what I was crying about."

Does this sound familiar? What has happened to this woman? How has she settled for "that which is not bread"? What part has the ad culture

played in her problem? Will a "new improved product" cure her blahs? Is she a candidate for women's liberation—or what?

4. Try the following as an effective discussion sparker or as a prayer of confession for a worship service:

Play Bach's "Jesu, Joy of Man's Desiring" on a record player. After thirty to sixty seconds, have a woman read the "blah's spot" over the music. Tape the two, either with the microphone picking up both sounds, or, if yours is a sophisticated machine, recording the music directly through a phonojack into the input of the recorder. Then go back and record the voice over the music using the sound-on-sound feature of the recorder. The contrast between Bach's great chorale of faith and the ad-culture woman's quiet despair makes for a thought-provoking presentation.

5. Read the Beatitudes in Matthew 5:3-11. If you can obtain the beautiful art print kit *Sister Corita*, place the Beatitudes mural on the wall. She calls these the "Happy Attitudes." Make a list of the

Happiness

Sought Throughout the Ages By Young, Old, Rich, and Poor.

WLIE CHANNEL 4
10:00 P.M.

The successful conclusion of an epic search brought to you by the United Ad Confederation

key word(s) in each "Happy Attitude," and beside it write the name of an advertised product with an appeal based on the opposite premise. In a third column try to find ads which affirm and support the Beatitude. Which is easier to complete—the first or second list?

6. For those who enjoy writing: rewrite the Beatitudes as "The Happy Attitudes for the Good Life," according to the Gospel of Madison Avenue. If you really get inspired, recast as much of the Sermon on the Mount as you can.

7. Make a list of all the commercials you can think of

that deal with women. What categories of women are portrayed in the ads? List the attributes of the ad culture's "ideal wife." Do you know anyone like this? What kind of a person is she as a spouse, mother, neighbor? What does she do with most of her time? Does she seem to be a whole or well-rounded human being? Or do certain attributes seem over emphasized?

8. Make a similar list of all the commercials you can recall involving men. If women appear in them, what roles do they play? How do they relate to men? (For example, study the coffee commercials.) What

WLIE: Channel 4

"PROMISES, PROMISES"

is the ad-culture man like? What kind of person is he at work, home, play?

9. Create a collage. Search through stacks of magazines for the ads of products which you have seen on television also. Make one or more collages on "The Good Life" as portrayed in the ads, and as suggested by the Sermon on the Mount. Each member could make his own, or by cutting out the side of a large appliance box, you will have a large enough area for the entire group to work on together. The artist of the group might work out a rough design as a guideline for the rest to follow. This will give the completed work more of an artistic unity than most amateur-created collage exhibits. However, don't let one person dominate this so much that the group's creativity is stifled.

Some variations of the above:

a. Gather eight to ten boxes of the same size (at least twelve-by-eighteen-by-twelve inches). Stack them in the shape of a cross from six to eight feet high. About two-thirds of the way up place a wide board to support the boxes that will form the transepts. Tape them all together with masking tape. On one side of the cross paste pictures and words from ads that deal with values and goals of "fallen man," the "old" man, or Adam (see Romans 7 for one of Paul's many discussions of this). On the opposite side use words and pictures from ads and old church school materials depicting the new creation in Christ. Have some jars or cans of poster paints and felt-tipped markers for the participants to use in creating their own designs over and around the paste-ons.

The cross collage can be set up near the beginning of a conference or retreat, and the participants can be encouraged to work on it at various free moments. This can be used as a focal point in the community's worship celebration. It worked very well at our church as a part of a family fun event. Adults and children pasted and painted at various times during the course of the evening, the result being a towering, eye-catching visual statement of the cross which added significantly to our closing worship.

b. If your local merchants are cooperative, you might be able to pick up their large signs, banners, and posters from displays left over from promotions. Parts or all of these can be taped up around the room, hung from the ceiling, or used to cover some of the boxes. A gas station owner once gave a number of his huge window banners to a church youth group; the ads declared, in beautiful biblical language, "We've Got the Spirit."

c. A Crawl-Thru Environment is also fun. This is made from old furniture and appliance cartons. On the outside paint and paste your designs dealing with the negative aspects of your theme—such as "The Good Life According to Madison Avenue." On the inside of the cartons "The Way of the Cross" could be depicted. Cut out windows and skylights in the boxes. Join several together. Let your imagination go—and have on hand plenty of masking tape, poster paints, brushes, felt-tipped markers, magazines, and paste.

I have been amazed at the beautiful results groups come up with. Some even filled their windows with simulated stained-glass designs. There have been windows cut in the shape of hearts and crosses; even pop-

style Sistine Chapel ceilings which you have to lie on your back to appreciate.

For an unusual effect, cut an opening three feet or more in one side of the carton and tape a "rear screen" over it. The material for the latter is fairly cheap; look for a shower curtain liner that has no pattern to it and is made of dull white transluscent plastic. Outside the carton set up a slide projector so that the slides, loaded in the tray backward, are focused on your rear screen window. If the projector has an automatic slide changer, use this so that no one will have to operate it all the time. As folk crawl through the environment, they will be surrounded by the art of their friends and also confronted by the constantly changing slides of the world outside.

10. Recycle television commercials. If you live in a community served by a local TV station, you might be able to secure some invaluable resources for study and worship. As was recommended earlier, check with the station management to see if they will give you their used commercials. These will come on small reels of 16mm film, usually marked

WLIE: Channel 4
"PROMISES, PROMISES"

with the product's and parent company's name—for example, Cheerios–General Mills. Sort them into piles of various categories, such as automotive products, cereals, beverages, foods, pet foods, patent medicines, public service spots, and so forth. To find out what is actually on them, you will either have to run them through a movie projector, or, for a quick check, to unwind the film and look at each scene as you hold it up against the light. A magnifying glass is helpful at this point. To rewind, just stick a pen or pencil through the hole of the reel and turn it quickly like a wheel. I'm assuming that you are not rich enough to own a 16mm film viewer-editor. If you can find one locally, however, try to borrow it.

Here are some possible uses for your collection of ads:

a. Select a number of spots to splice together whole. Rewind them on a larger reel (most photo supply stores sell extra 16mm film reels that will hold from 400 to 1,200 feet), and you will have five or more minutes of commercials that you can view and discuss at any time. This could be useful for additional sessions on values clarification, studies of mass media or film-making techniques, or as part of a multimedia show.

b. As you look through the films, cut out those scenes which will fit your study or worship theme. For instance, if yours is "joy," look for scenes of people having a good time, smiling, eating, celebrating. Such scenes are plentiful in the ads for foods, beverages, toys, and a host of other products. Arrange them in the order you want, then time them, if you plan to use them with an accompanying tape of music and sound effects. A rough way to do this before splicing the clips together is to mark off a stick or piece of cardboard for every six frames of the film; 16mm film runs through the projector at the rate of 24 frames per second, so by laying your film clip along side your "ruler," you can tell how long the scene is. For example, one that is ninety frames long will be three and three-fourths seconds long.

Add slides to your completed film, a tape of music, and you will have an exciting multimedia show at very little cost, especially if you use mostly the homemade lift-off slides created from old magazines and slick-paper catalogues.

c. Ads can become a prayer of confession. Select several of the more obnoxious ones, and splice them together in the order that best fits your purpose. Ask the creative writers in your group to write a response as if God were talking back to the ads or to the people in them. Encourage the group to experiment with this. Some members might want to use part of the soundtrack of the film and then turn the sound down for their own response. Others might create an entirely new soundtrack of music and words. Still others might show the ads right through as they are, and then respond. Turn loose those interested in such a project, equip them with the necessary supplies and gadgets, and you will be surprised at what they do—and possibly very moved when such a confession is used as part of a worship service.

Celebrating with Gusto: Some Worship Suggestions

As with the other study sessions, it would be appropriate to close with an act of celebrating the good news. The following is offered to stimulate your ideas. It could be used in its entirety at a retreat or conference, or portions might be suitable for a shorter session.

Prelude: Play the recording of Simon and Garfunkel's "The Sounds of Silence."

Call to Worship: Isaiah 55:1-2, read either by the leader or responsively by the community.

Song/Act of Praise

Act of Confession:

Option 1. Play a series of the soundtracks of ads which you have edited for the sake of brevity. Allow a pause on the tape between each ad for the people to respond with such words as, "Good Lord, forgive us."

Option 2. Play your recording, or do it live, of "Jesu, Joy of Man's Desiring" and the housewife (see Probe No. 4).

Option 3. Place a stack of products advertised on TV (actually, you need only the containers in which they are packaged) upon the communion table in place of, or in front of, the cross so that it appears that we are worshiping them. Write an appropriate prayer or litany.

WLIE: Channel 4

"PROMISES, PROMISES"

Option 4. Use the film-confession described in Probe No. 10-C.

Option 5. If you have made the cross collage described earlier, have the "sin" side facing the congregation. Use a prayer which has come out of your session together, or if the members of the community feel free enough, the leader could invite them to share those areas of their lives in which they need God's healing forgiveness.

Option 6. Show your reel of TV commercials. Start out with the soundtrack of the film, but after a minute or so slowly turn it down and bring up the volume level of a tape recorder, on which you have a tape of Simon and Garfunkel's "Big Bright Green Pleasure Machine" and "The Sounds of Silence."

The Assurance of God's Pardon/Love:

Option 1. If Option 1, 2, 4, or 6 is chosen for an act of confession, write a matching assurance based on an appropriate scripture passage.

Option 2. For Option 3, one of the worship leaders should sweep away the products from before the cross while another person gives the assurance (perhaps based on Philippians 3:7-11, Phillips translation).

Option 3. If Option 5 is used, turn the cross collage around to expose the "new creation" side as the assurance based on II Corinthians 5 is read. If physical conditions allow, you could have the people sitting on the floor on one side of the cross, and then invite them to get up and move around to the other side. ("Pick up your life and walk, for the Christ who healed the lame continues to forgive our sins and to invite us to share in his new creation.")

Act of Praise: A hymn, doxology, Gloria, or a dance interpretation.

A good traditional hymn that will be unconventional if used at this point, especially if it's not December, is the third stanza of "Joy to the World."

Reading: Any Scripture passage dealing with values

(Some examples: Mark 10:17-22; Matthew 5:3-16; 6:19-21, 24-34; 16:24-26.)

The Preached/Acted-Out Word: Share your multimedia or slide show.

Act out or pantomime one of the parables such as the rich young ruler or the rich fool.

Select one of the excellent readings from the book *Discovery in Advertising,* or portions of T. S. Eliott's poem "The Hollow

Men" or Chorus III from his "Choruses from 'The Rock.'"
Include some of your thoughts on values.

Responding to the Word:

Prayer: Share concerns.

Credo: Let those who wish complete the statement "I believe
that the most important thing in life is _____."

Or let the members share their interpretations of their
collages.

Those who have worked on the Crawl-Thru Environment
might have kept the inside of their project secret until now,
thus heightening the curiosity of the rest of the group. They
could lead the rest of the group through at this time on a
sort of "faith journey."

Closing: Share an act of dedication and the Passing of the
Peace.

KKID: Channel 5—
"Suffer the Little Children . . ."

Children's Programming and the Kingdom

"And Now a Word from . . ."

No area of television programming better shows the depth to which the medium can sink or the height to which it can rise than so-called children's TV. The first big hit on TV was a children's program called "Howdy Doody" in 1947. Some critics would say that this began the downward plunge that's continued almost unabated ever since. They claim that Saturday morning is the time to sell toys and cereals that are almost as inferior as the programs they sponsor. And yet such good shows as "The Big Blue Marble," "Mister Rogers," and "The Electric Company" also are aired on Saturdays. Your probe of children and television will be further complicated by the fact that children's viewing is not confined just to "kiddies' shows." Since TV comes into the home, they watch many of the programs which their parents tune in—Westerns, adventure stories, quiz shows, and, of course, commercials. The King James version of Jesus' famous invitation takes on new meaning when we consider what such exposure might be doing to and for them: "Suffer the little children to come . . ."

For the Leader

1. After deciding on the exercises and options you hope to cover, make the as-

signments called for at least a week in advance.

2. Tape the "And Now a Word from . . ." segments.

3. Your group might not include parents, so when you read "your child" or "your children," think of brothers or sisters or children you know.

4. Decorate your meeting room with some of the bright, childlike posters available from Abbey Press or Argus Communications, balloons, streamers, and homemade banners.

5. Have on hand tapes and cassette; Bibles; copies of this book; crayons and paper; a record player and the songs "Both Sides Now" (recorded by Judy Collins), "Children Live What They Learn" (Les Crane), and "Everything Is Beautiful" (Ray Stevens); and copies of *The Genesis Songbook.*

KKID: Channel 5
"SUFFER THE CHILDREN"

For the Group

1. **Option a.** *A Fantasy Trip–Re-entering Childhood.*

The leader asks participants to take off their shoes and lie down on the floor. The room should be large enough so that no one is touching anyone else. Play a children's album of songs—maybe one of Mr. Rogers'. Everyone should close his eyes while listening to the songs. After a few minutes the leader should gradually turn the volume down while saying something like the following:

"Your eyes are closed . . . We want to take a trip . . . Each one's trip will be different, yet similar. I want you to think back to the time when you were a child. Think of any age before you were nine or

Captain Kangaroo

Mr. Rogers

KKID: Channel 5

"SUFFER THE CHILDREN"

ten [pause for several moments]. Zero in now on one particular time ... How old are you? ... What is your favorite toy? What does it feel like? Look like? Smell like? Where is your favorite place in your house? In your neighborhood? What songs do you like? Do you have any pets? What is your favorite entertainment? ... Movies, radio, television? Who is your favorite hero or heroine? What do you want to do the most? Become the most? When you look at clouds, what do you see?

After a few moments, during which the leader invites the group to return their thoughts to the present, divide into groups of four and share your fantasy trip. How do you feel about it? About your childhood?

Option b. Play the Joni Mitchell song "Both Sides Now"—Judy Collins' version is best for this. Ask the group to listen closely to the words. Then play the song again at a lower volume level and ask: How did you look at clouds when you were a child? Did you ever play the cloud game? Can you recall when you were first smitten with someone of the opposite sex? How did you feel

toward that person? Toward yourself? Are you as full of wonder now as you were as a child? As full of trust? As idealistic? As hopeful?

After the song ends have someone read from Mark 10:13-16. What elements of childhood do the songwriter and Jesus value? What seems to happen to these as we grow older?

2. Some groups might want to begin this session here rather than probing their own childhood and feelings. Note that there are two options.

Option a. Invite a few children to meet with you for a few minutes. An adult enjoying good rapport with children should sit on the floor with them and ask such questions as the following:

Why do you watch TV? What do you like the best about it? What do you dislike the most? What program(s) do you like the best? Why? Do you know how long you watch TV each day? What other things do you like to do? Would you rather do them or watch TV? What do you like the most on Saturdays—the shows with real people, or the cartoons? Why? If you could make your own TV program what kind would it be? Describe it.

Option b. Ask three or four members, armed with the above questions, to talk with several children during the week before this session. Have them record the children's answers on a cassette tape recorder. Each interviewer can give a report summarizing the responses and play the tape of one or two of the most interesting answers.

3. **Option a.** Let those who have watched specific children's shows share their findings with the group. Describe the shows and include answers to the following:

Is there anything unique about the show? Does the producer seem to have a high regard for the intelligence of children? How realistic are the plots and the

acting? Are the characters believable? Is the emphasis on action, even violence? Are alternatives to violence suggested? What values does the show teach? (Go beneath the facile "right triumphs over wrong" formula. *How* does right win out?)

Option b. Video tape portions of several children's shows and play them back for the group.

"And Now a Word from . . ."

I don't know who first made the comparison, but I remember reading once about Popeye and Casper as two ways of facing life. Both characters have been popular with children of all ages, first in comic strips, then in movies, and over the years on televi-

KKID: Channel 5

sion. After a slow start, when the villain has the upper hand, Popeye ingests his spinach, is endowed with super strength, and promptly beats the brains out of his hapless opponent. Popeye has a "beat the hell out of 'em" approach to life. On the other hand, Casper, "the friendly ghost," is just that. Through his wits and good nature he tries to overcome the hostility of his opponent. He destroys his enemies by making them into friends. If at times he was a little syrupy-sweet, his adventures at least provided a contrast to the usual cartoon violence.

4. Have you seen any other cartoons which follow Casper's lead in suggesting that force and violence are not the only ways of dealing with enemies? Do your children *like* Casper? Or would they rather see a "socko-wham" show?

5. Another interesting contrast is that between two popular kiddie shows—"Captain Kangaroo" and "Mister Rogers' Neighborhood."

a. Watch the two programs. What seems to be their view of children? Compare their styles.

b. Both are educational; which seems to dwell more on facts, and which on relationships and self-awareness?

6. In children's adventure shows, what qualities of the hero are emphasized? How are women and girls portrayed? Are they seen as perpetual victims needing to be rescued? Are they more squeamish or nagging? Do they need frequent correcting by, or help from, males? What are the villains like? Any stereotyping, racial or otherwise? Is the villian the stock kind who wants to take over the world for his own fiendish glee? How many female villains can you think of?

7. What alternatives to cartoons and adventure stories are offered by your stations? Do any of these help awaken a sense of wonder or stimulate a child's imagination? Do any of them cause him/her to turn off the set and investigate or try out something?

"And Now a Word from . . ."

Long before television the Hebrew-Christian tradition recognized the importance of the child's environment and early training. From Deuteronomy and Proverbs to the Gospels and Epistles, much emphasis is placed upon the necessity to "train up a child in the way he should go." Jesus emphasized the enormous responsibility of this task when he declared that "whoever causes one of these little ones who believe in me to sin, it would be better for him to have a great millstone fastened around his neck and to be drowned in the depth of the sea." He was also concerned that those who train up a child might train *out* of him some important qualities that are necessary if he is to be a whole person—qualities such as wonder, joy, and trust. The Master once declared that "whoever does not receive the kingdom of God like a child shall not enter it."

8. Read Luke's version of the blessing of the children (Luke 18:15-17). Note the parable in verses 9-14. Why do you think the disciples tried to keep the children away? What do you think Jesus meant when he said that we must receive the Kingdom like a little child? Compare the disciples' attitudes toward children to his.

This incident is followed in Luke by the encounter with the rich young ruler. Read this, and compare this man's attitude to what Jesus has said about childlikeness.

9. If you did not play the song "Both Sides Now" at the beginning, play it now, after you have passed out crayons and paper. Ask the group to draw/sketch/write their reaction to the song. In groups of four, have each person share

KKID: Channel 5
"SUFFER THE CHILDREN"

his/her interpretation. Compare the song to Luke 18:15-17. Close with sentence prayers for the Spirit to nurture or restore the child within us.

Or, listen to the song-poem "Children Live What They Learn." Someone should read Matthew 18:1-6 for the group. Close with sentence prayers for our children and the child within us all.

Further Probes

1. Read Matthew 18:1-6. Jesus strongly emphasizes the responsibility of those who come into contact with children. What do you think about his statement?

Your child might have been baptized or dedicated shortly after birth. If so, you made a promise to raise your child in a Christian manner, as Paul put it, "in the nurture and admonition of the Lord." How might your guidance of your child's TV viewing be part of fulfilling such a pledge?

Play "Children Live What They Learn." How do the programs which your child watches jibe with the lines in the poem about hostility, ridicule, tolerance, and approval? Does his/her TV viewing reinforce the claim that he/she is a "child of the universe"?

2. Probing some specific shows:

KKID: Channel 5

"SUFFER THE CHILDREN"

a. What is the "Wonderful World of Disney" like? Describe the Disney view of life and death, sin and salvation. Are the characters and situations believable? Some critics claim that the "true life" nature films sacrifice truth for cutesy entertainment. React to this charge.

b. What do the Peanuts Specials reveal about children and their world? Is it always sweet and innocent? Give some examples. If you are using this book in December, be sure to watch the annual Christmas show. If not, this episode is available in book form.

How are Charlie and the little tree alike? Compare them with the figure described in Isaiah 53. What changes the attitude of the gang toward the tree—and toward Charlie? What changes the attitude of mankind toward the crucified Jesus and his cross? Imagine the mixed feelings of the wise men leaving Herod's sumptuous palace to find the infant Jesus in a peasant's rude hut.

Ask for volunteers to act out a similar scene in which the three Wise Guys—Schroeder, Linus, and Lucy—are engaged in a long search; when they arrive at their destination they find Charlie Brown and his scraggly little Christmas tree.

c. Many of Dr. Seuss's strange, funny poems and stories, like the biblical parables or Aesop's Fables, contain some important lessons. Anyone working with or concerned for children should turn on to these modern parables, especially the annual Christmas showing of *The Day the Grinch Stole Christmas.* This story is also available in book form.

Describe the life-style of the Grinch and the townspeople of Whosville. What reaction did the Grinch expect from his theft of the presents? What was his understanding of Christmas? Discuss the line, "Maybe Christmas doesn't come from a store, maybe Christmas is something more." How is the Grinch like King Herod, the rich young ruler, the rich fool, us?

3. Do you think that your church and church school leaders understand the TV generation? Attending your worship service and church school classes, would a child see any relationship between the world of faith and the world of television? How?

4. If you invited children to come to this session(s), here is a list of some further activities.

Option a. Sing, hum, or play on the piano the opening lines of six to eight of the great hymns of the church. How many do they recognize? Now do the same with the opening part of the same number of TV commercial songs. How many of these do they recognize?

Option b. Divide the children and an equal number of adult volunteers into groups of four. Don't mix children and adults in the groups. Distribute crayons and paper. Each group's task is to draw or design a product that will be advertised for children on Saturday morning. Write the commercial, complete with jingle or song if you can. Make the product as outlandish or silly as you wish—only your commercial must present it as the greatest product ever offered. Flip a coin as to whether the children or the adults go first to present their ad to the others. If the children are a little shy at trying this at first, an adult might help them get started.

Option c. Ask someone in advance to tape a number of children's ads. Listen to them together, and ask the

children to respond to such questions as: What things are being advertised? What did the TV-man promise you about the thing? Are the toys that you buy in the store really as exciting as they looked on TV? Were you ever disappointed by the toy? Can you always believe what you hear or see on TV? Why?

5. In small groups think of creative ways to interpret a Bible story to children via such approaches as: "Kukla, Fran and Ollie," "The Three Stooges" or "I Love Lucy," "Sesame Street," "Electric Company," or a science fiction show.

If you can't think of a story, try Jacob and Esau, Jonah, Moses and the burning bush, Moses and Pharaoh.

6. If you have access to TV commercials (see the last part of Channel 4 for details on obtaining these), splice together several children's ads. These might be spots for toys, breakfast cereals, or candy. Work out your own soundtrack, perhaps using some of the songs mentioned earlier, Bible verses, and narrative.

7. Tape the audio portions of a number of children's shows and ads. Listen to these. Choose a theme, perhaps suggested by something on your tape, the songs

KKID: Channel 5
"SUFFER THE CHILDREN"

discussed earlier, or a Bible passage—such as trust, love, openness, holding onto a sense of wonder. Select portions of your taped shows, rearranging them to suit your theme, and add your own music or narrative where needed. Make a master tape of this.

Others could be creating slides to go with this, the result being an intriguing statement about life, God, or the child within us.

Celebrating as Children of the Universe:

Prelude: Play the record "Everything Is Beautiful."
Call to Worship:

> **Leader**—Come and see the world which God has created.
>
> **People**—For its blues, reds, yellows, and greens, we praise you, O God.
>
> **Leader**—Come and hear the sounds of the Lord's world.
>
> **People**—For its roars, its music, its gentle sounds, and still silences, we thank you, O Lord.
>
> **Leader**—Come and touch the marvelous wonders God's fingers have fashioned.
>
> **People**—For the rough and smooth textures, for warm and cool surfaces, for tickly and tingly feelings, we celebrate your name, O God.
>
> **Leader**—Come on tiptoe to taste and smell the goodness of the Creator's universe.
>
> **People**—For the joys of all the senses we sing and shout our praises to you, Creator of the universe.

Song of Praise: "Joyful, Joyful We Adore Thee" or "Morning Has Broken"
Call to Confession: Read Mark 10:13-16 and/or play "Both Sides Now."

> **All**—Forgive us, Lord, for our super-sophistication that shuts out the child within ourselves and others; for walking through your multicolored world with blind eyes; for being too busy or self-important to stop and smell your roses; for all which we have done to diminish wonder, trust, and joy; in the name of that first Child of the universe, we pray. Amen.
>
> **Leader**—In Christ you are a new creation; the old passes away, the new has come. Look with new eyes. Listen with new ears. Come and see the world which the Creator has made, for you

are children of the universe. (Play the chorus of "You Are a Child of the Universe" from *Desiderata.*)

Reading: Psalm 150

Meditation: Let those who prepared a film, tape collage, or a slide show share this.

A Time of Sharing:

Leader—"O taste, and see that the Lord is good." Pass around a box of graham crackers, cookies, or animal crackers, or a basket of apples or peaches. Share a pitcher of Kool-Aid. Let those who wish, imagine that they are a child for the first time tasting such foods. Share your reactions with the group as part of a group prayer of thanksgiving.

Song: "Take a Giant Step," "I'd Like to Teach the World to Sing," or "Thank You, Thank You Lord" (Avery and Marsh)

WYUK: Channel 6— "A Laughing Matter"

Situation Comedies and the Gospel

"And Now a Word from . . ."

Situation comedies have been important to television ever since "The Goldbergs" started audiences laughing in 1949. These shows range from the banal to the brilliant, but all have one thing in common— they attempt to make us laugh at the human situation, even if the producer has to add canned laughter to make sure we get the point. They also possess another common element—they tend to keep coming back from Cancellation Cemetery. They neither die nor, like old soldiers, fade away, at least not for long if they were once successful. They soon join the rerun circuit. On a hot summer's night in Pittsburgh, the viewer could see only four new "sit-coms" being shown again. However, if he had been willing to start watching at 7:30 A.M., he could have seen over *twenty* episodes of older series. Chances are that you can watch an episode from a majority of the shows that were popular as long ago as fifteen years. So turn on your set and start laughing.

For the Leader

1. Check over the questions and exercises you hope to cover, making any assignments necessary.

2. Tape the "And Now a Word from . . ." segments.

3. If you include the guess-

ing game (#2), have enough stick-on name tags for everyone. Mark these with the names of well-known situation comedy characters.

4. Have on hand: tape and cassette, Bibles, copies of this book, and *TV Guide* magazine. Possibly a record player and the albums *Godspell* and *For Heaven's Sake*.

5. For your own preparation, a reading of Nelvin Vos's little book *For God's Sake, Laugh!* would be helpful. This contains some fascinating insights into a theology of laughter.

For the Group

1. Turn on your set and watch part or all of a situation comedy. Or show a previously

WYUK: Channel 6
"A LAUGHING MATTER"

recorded videotape of one or a collection of segments from several different kinds. Ask some questions for probing them: What class of society are the characters from? What is their home like? If a family, do the children act like ones you know? Do they spend their time watching as much TV? Are the characters open and honest with one another? Or does the situation and humor depend upon deception? What is the problem? Is the solution convincing? Does the "all's well that ends well" conclusion ever give the impression that the end justifies the means?

2. Divide into groups of four to six. The leader will come around and place a name tag on the back of one member of each group. The name of a situation comedy (sit-com) character will be on the tag. The others should give nonverbal clues as the tagged person tries to guess who he/she is. These clues can be mannerisms such as the character's walk, hair style, facial expressions, type of clothing, or whatever. Each member of the group should get the chance to be tagged. Only as a last resort should a verbal clue, such as the character's favorite expression, be given.

3. Stay in your small

WYUK: Channel 6

"A LAUGHING MATTER"

groups while the leader passes out copies of *TV Guide* magazine. Look through the listing of situation comedies and choose the character with whom you most identify. After a couple of minutes, share your characters with one another and tell why you chose him or her. What makes this character or the situation funny?

Share the funniest thing that ever happened to you. Was it funny to you at the time it happened? If not, what enabled you to change your view?

"And Now a Word from . . ."

Often comedy results from the gap between our pretensions and reality. The child dressed up in Mom's clothing parades solemnly into the living room. We suppress our smiles, perhaps, so as not to hurt her feelings. An older, but less tactful, brother or sister bursts into laughter. Lucy tries to join Ricky's nightclub act, and winds up making a shambles of the nightclub and band.

Something of this kind of humor can be seen frequently in the Scriptures. The Pharisees, protectors of the law, love to parade around with holy, righteous airs. In reality, Jesus claims, they are "like whitewashed tombs, which outwardly appear beautiful, but within they are full of dead men's bones and all uncleanness." The distance of time and overlaid layers of piety have blinded us to the humor of the Bible, but it's there, reminding us that "he who sits in the heavens laughs." The human situation, despite all evidence to the contrary, is not a tragedy, but a comedy—a divine comedy.

4. Here are some Bible passages wherein humor is an important factor. Try to approach them fresh as if you were hearing the story for the first time. Since there are too many to examine, pick out just the ones that seem most interesting. Or stay in your small

"A LAUGHING MATTER"

groups, let each group pick two or three passages, then come back and share your findings with the others. If time allows, work out a skit based on one of the passages.

a. Numbers 22:15-35—the story of Balaam and his ass. Balaam is supposed to be a great diviner or sorcerer, but who is it that first sees the angel of the Lord? Imagine the Hebrews telling this story around their campfires.

b. Isaiah 44:9-20—a funny put-down of idolatry. This is a very daring, even dangerous passage. Look up the setting of the passage in a modern Bible commentary. Where were the Hebrews, including the writer, when this passage was written? Whose god seemed to be the strongest at the time? Why was the passage written?

c. Psalm 2—the high and the mighty versus God. The writer compares the pretensions of the lordly and pompous rulers of earth to the hidden power of God. Why might this have been a good passage to read at the inaugurations of a couple of our past presidents?

d. Matthew 6:2—blowing your own horn. Just close your eyes and imagine the scene.

e. Matthew 6:5-7—empty prayers. This provides more grist for the imagination. Write out the kind of "prayer to the great god—Me" Jesus is referring to.

f. Matthew 6:16—fellowship of the long face. Picture Jesus' expression as he is speaking, or imagine Ted Baxter of "The Mary Tyler Moore Show" as the one who is fasting.

g. Matthew 7:1-5—speck-removing in a log jam. What a basis for an episode from "All In the Family," "The Odd

WYUK: Channel 6

"A LAUGHING MATTER"

Couple," or "The Mary Tyler Moore Show"! What character would be the speck-remover?

h. Matthew 19:23-24—needling the rich. The aftermath of the visit of the rich young ruler produces a humorous picture, perhaps a different way of saying "you can't take it with you."

i. Matthew 23—humor turns sour. The occasion is loaded with danger, the speaker's intentions are deadly serious—yet can you still find a few touches of humor or irony in the chapter? Picture a "Mary Tyler Moore" episode with Mary turning on Ted, Phyllis, or Sue Ann in such a fashion.

"And Now a Word from . . ."

Comedy also is produced by incongruity—two diverse elements placed together. For example, a dignified-looking man in a top hat, monocle, and tuxedo walks into the room and waves his umbrella at us. We look at him and laugh—for we see that he's not wearing any pants. He looks down at his polka-dotted shorts and asks, "What's the matter? I bought these at the finest store in town!" We laugh again. Or a dog walks into the room and we look up. If it's our living room we merely greet it, but if the room is our church sanctuary, then we might laugh. The dog returns—this time walking on hind legs and dressed in a suit. We probably laugh no matter where we are. The element of surprise—expecting one thing and discovering something else—keeps comedy fresh and varied. Add this to the traditional view in drama that a comedy is "all's well that ends well" and you have another element of the situation comedy. You also have an important element of the gospel of Jesus Christ. The four Gospels are closer in spirit to a situation comedy than to a Greek tragedy. Tragic man has done his worst in crucifying the Son of God—but the crucified One is also the risen One. Lucy, Gomer Pyle, and even Gilligan are closer to the gospel than we usually suspect.

5. Do you think that most people look at the story of Jesus as a tragedy or as a comedy? What basic element makes it a comedy?

Read John's version of the trial of Jesus in chapters 18

WYUK: Channel 6
"A LAUGHING MATTER"

and 19. On the surface who has the power and trappings of high office? In reality who is in control of the situation? How are Pilate and the priests like children in dress-up clothing? Compare this scene to Jesus' words in Matthew 10:24-39.

6. Read Romans 8:31-39; I Corinthians 4:7-15; and Philippians 1:12-14; 1:19-21; 3:8-9; 4:10-13. How do we usually view such events? What has happened to Paul that he is not broken up by such happenings?

Close this session by singing or listening to "Lord of the Dance." The first exercise in "Further Probes" would also be a fitting way to close this session.

WYUK: Channel 6

"A LAUGHING MATTER"

Further Probes

1. The musical play *Godspell* treats the Gospel of Matthew as a comedy. Let those who have seen the play or movie describe some of the ways that the life and teachings of Christ were presented in a vaudeville, musical comedy style. Play and discuss the song "You Are the Light of the World" from the album. Compare the viewpoint of *Godspell* with that of *Jesus Christ: Superstar.*

2. Another comical approach to the gospel is the older musical *For Heaven's Sake.* Play and discuss the song "He Was a Flop at Thirty-three." Why is this "successful man's" view of Jesus so funny?

3. Some situation comedies, especially the earlier ones, deal with problems as weighty as whether junior should pick his pimple or not, and if he does, will it spoil his date? Others venture into more promising territory and deal with social issues or genuine problems of human relationships. Be sure to watch and discuss such programs as the original "Dick Van Dyke Show," "The Mary Tyler Moore Show," "The Bob Newhart Show," "Rhoda," "Maude," "The Jeffersons," "Chico and the Man," "M.A.S.H.," and of course, "All in the Family."

Look through *TV Guide* magazine for others.

Some church groups have taped such shows and played them back on Sunday mornings for discussion. A study of values, communication, interpersonal relations, or transactional analysis would be greatly enriched by viewing such shows.

4. Divide into groups of four to six and create a skit based on a biblical story as an episode from a popular situation comedy. Some suggestions are Adam and Eve, Abraham and Sarah and the birth of Isaac (Genesis 18:1-15; 21:1-7), Jacob and Esau, Balaam and his ass, Jonah, the parables of Jesus. For a sterling example of the transformation of Jesus' parable of the Pharisee and the Publican (Luke 18:9-14) into an episode for "A Fall in the Family," see the script at the end of this chapter. This may take some time, so plan accordingly. Agree to reassemble at a designated time to share your masterpieces. Just hearing what story and TV program each group combined should be fun.

5. During the week or two before this session, tape a number of shows. Many of these rely on dialogue for humor as much as the video, so you might not lose too

"A LAUGHING MATTER"

much of the comedy with just the audio. Select the best lines from several shows and dub them onto another tape. Insert suitable narrative, biblical passages, or music for a funny but pointed lesson. For example:

Read first	then dub in sounds of
"Blessed are those who mourn . . .	Lucy or Gloria crying
Blessed are the meek . . .	Ted Baxter boasting
Blessed are those who hunger and thirst for righteousness . . .	George Jefferson
Blessed are the merciful . . .	Maude declaring, "God'll get you for that!"
Blessed are the pure in heart . . .	Georgette Baxter (of "MTM")
Blessed are the peacemakers . . .	Edith Bunker
Blessed are those who are persecuted . . .	Gilligan or Gomer Pyle
Blessed are you when men revile you."	Lucy Carmichael and her boss; or Archie berating Edith.

Other Scripture passages that could be interspersed with such voice tracks are the Ten Commandments, some proverbs, or portions of the Sermon on the Mount.

6. You can add slides to the above to create a slide show for a funny-serious program at a family night supper. It's not too difficult to photograph the images on your TV screen, especially if you have a single-lens reflex camera and a color set. Load your camera with high-speed Ektachrome film, and turn the TV set's contrast knob so that the most detail can be seen. Set your shutter speed at no faster than 1/8 second and the lens opening at f/2.8 to f4, depending on the brightness of the image. A built-in light meter is a great help here. Be sure to turn off the room lights and position the set so that no reflections from windows or other light sources are caught on the surface of the screen. You are shooting an available light scene, so do *not* use a flash or flood light!

Thus you can build a collection of slides of TV characters to show during the appropriate part of your sound track. For a strange or surrealistic effect, mix in slides of war, racism, poverty, and pollution.

WYUK: Channel 6
"A LAUGHING MATTER"

Scenes Based on Luke 18:9-14 for "A Fall in the Family"

The scene opens with Arnie and Enid Clunker passing through the doors of a church.

Enid: Arnie, I'm so glad you've agreed to come to church with me today.

Arnie: Yeah—yeah, Enid. I guess you should be. But it *is* Easter, and I figure I owes the Lord something—at least I ought to be willing to suffer through another of the Reverend Belcher . . .

Enid: It's Felcher, Arnie.

Arnie: Yeah, well, whatever. As I said, I oughta be willing to suffer through Fletcher's sermon at least once a year.

(They pause at the entrance to the sanctuary.)

Arnie: Geez—look at dem guys all dressed up like dey was at a funeral or wedding!

Enid: Shhh, Arnie . . .

(She points to an inscription in Gothic letters over the entrance way.)

Arnie: Whaddaya want, Enid? Oh—ya wants me to read that perscription up there—Geez, I don't blame you—the creep that done that sure can't write good—I wouldn't hire him for nothing. Let's see—it says L-E-T—Let—A-L-L—all—T-H-E—the—E-A-R-T-H—urth—K-E-E

Enid: Shhh–Arnie–we're in . . .

WYUK: Channel 6
"A LAUGHING MATTER"

Arnie: Damn it, Enid—I'm trying to read the sign fer you. Let's see—K-E-E-P—keep—S-I-L-E-N-C-E. Now what the hell does *that* spell—Sie—Linz—Oh, *silence*—Hey, that's a fancy description that says "Shut up." Well, why didn't you tell me, Enid?

(An usher hands them a bulletin.)

Arnie: Hey, ⁻look at this, Enid—this is printed. The old church must be doing pretty well.

(They take their seats about halfway down, Arnie stepping on feet, almost falling, looking at the people as if it were their fault and not his, Enid demurely following, apologizing for her husband. As they sit she almost hides or crawls into the bulletin. Arnie, oblivious to the commotion he has caused, looks all around the sanctuary.)

Arnie: *(A little bit quieter, but not much):* Say, Enid, this joint's packed almost as much as Kelsey's Bar used to be on fight night . . . What the—do you see what I see, sittin' two rows ahead just as big as you please—a colored man and woman!?

Enid: Shhh, Arnie—someone will hear you.

Arnie: What do I care? I'm telling you there's coloreds sittin' up there as if they belonged here! What's the church coming to anyway? Lettin' coloreds come in—don't they have their own church?

Enid: But Arnie, that's the Turners. They joined the church since the last time you was here—last Easter.

Arnie: I don't care who they are. It ain't right mixin' the races. If God intended it to be that way, he'd of made us all white. Of all places to go against the Lord—why it'll lead to misimpregnation or worse; I oughta go down and . . .

Enid: No you won't, Arnie. The Turners are part of this church—maybe more than you are, since they're here every Sunday—and more . . .

(The sound of the organ and choir swell up.)

(Fade out to black.)

(Fade in on the Clunker's home. Mack and Glory greet their parents as the older couple come in the door.)

Glory: Hi, Mom. Hi, Daddy. How was church?

Arnie: Yahh—don't ask me. Get out of my way, Meathead!

(He goes up the stairs hurriedly. We hear bathroom sounds.)

Mack: What happened, Mom?

WYUK: Channel 6

"A LAUGHING MATTER"

Didn't our saint enjoy his day in church? Wasn't the service any good?

Enid: Oh, the service was just fine—so much pretty music and all. Gladys Tremble sang a solo with the choir. You know Gladys—she has such a fine . . .

Glory: Mom, will you get on with what happened?

Enid: Oh, yeah—well—everything was fine—but your father, he got kind of upset. The Turners were there—

Mack: That's the black couple you were telling us about that joined last year?

Enid: Yeah, that's them. "As black as spades," Arnie says. Well, I seen him get all mad inside—you know how your father does—but I took hold of his arm and by the time the choir and Reverend Felcher come in he's a little calmer and the service starts. Only I can tell Arnie ain't entirely calm cause he's singing . . .

Mack: What's wrong with that?

Enid: You ever hear Arnie sing at the top of his lungs? Six people in the rows ahead of us turned around. Well, we got through the hymn and a prayer and then came a prayer of confession—one of those printed kind—and Arnie kept talking under his breath saying he hadn't done nothing to ask forgiveness for. The prayer talked about hating our brother and stuff like that.

Mack: Yeah, Arnie's never done *that*—he won't admit that any of us *are* his brothers.

Glory: Mack! Go on, Ma.

Enid: Well, just as we're finishing that prayer a young man comes in. He's dressed in one of those African dakiris . . .

Glory: Dashiki, Ma.

Enid: Yeah, one of them, and his hair is as long as those pictures of Jesus. Well, Arnie takes one look at him—he's coming down the pew to take the empty spot next to us—and he says something like "No wierdo pinko's goin' to set next to me," and he goes out the other way. Fortunately we're standing anyway and singing the Gloria Patri—say, ain't that nice? I never noticed before. That song has your name in it.

Glory: Ma, go on!

Enid: Sure, sure Glory. Well, Arnie moves out to the aisle. He waved to me, only I won't move. I think to myself—now if I was that person how would I feel if someone started to move when I came in—so I shake my head and stay. So Arnie gives me one of those signs of his and goes on to find another seat. I can tell he ain't very happy cause he can't find anything but a seat up on the front row.

Mack: *(Laughs.)* Can you imagine, Arnie on the front row in church? That would interfere with his sleeping.

Enid: Mack, that ain't fair. Arnie don't sleep in church. Just dozes a little now and then. Well, later during the announcements, Reverend Felcher greets us all and jokes about how glad he is to see all us sinners in church on Easter, only I don't think Arnie took it as a joke.

Glory: Why not, Ma?

Enid: Cause he was looking straight at your father when he said it. And then he read from the Bible—from the Gospel of Luke about two men that went to the temple to . . .

Glory: Ma, you don't have to tell us everything! Just the parts that're important.

Enid: But this part is. You see, it's about two people who went to the big church in Jerusalem. One of them was a Parsi or something, and he thanked God that he was there and told the Lord how much money he gave the church and how good he had been. And then he saw

the other man, a Republican—they was bad people in those days . . .

Mack: Some of them haven't done too well today, either.

Enid: Well, when this good man saw the bad man there in church he said how glad he was that he wasn't like him. And the Republican, he wouldn't even look up at God—he just said, "Please, Mr. God, be merciful to me a sinner!" Well, Mr. Felcher spoke on the meaning of that—and I could tell that the young man that had come in was really listening, cause a couple of times he wiped his eyes, and he nodded his head.

Mack: Maybe he was dozing off like Arnie.

Enid: No—no, it wasn't like Arnie cause his eyes was open and he was smiling. He was agreeing or something. Well, after the long prayer and offering and a hymn we was leaving. I waited for Arnie and asked him if he enjoyed the service only he won't hardly speak to me. He says something like Reverend Felcher oughta mind his own business. And then he tries to sneak around the line at the door shaking the minister's hand. But Reverend Felcher sees us and calls over, "Good morning, Mr. and Mrs. Clunker. It's so

good to see you here today."
Only Arnie just snorts and
leaves me there to say good-
bye to the Reverend.

*(The sound of the toilet
flushing. All look up the
stairs as Arnie descends.)*

Mack: Hi, Arn. I hear you had a
great time in church.

Arnie: Oh yeah, wise guy?
Well, let me tell you, I ain't
going back there. I had a
helluva time. Couldn't set
next to yer Ma—and she
won't move to find a place
where we can both sit. And
then their allowing all kinds
of characters that don't belong there to come in. I ain't
got nothin' against the coloreds, but you'd think that
on Easter they'd want to go
to their own church—and
that long-haired wierdo-
creepo-pinko who barged in
dressed in those clothes
only queers and dope ad-
dicts wear.

Glory: Oh, Daddy, what difference does it make what he
looks like as long as he's
there?

Arnie: It makes plenty of difference to *me,* little girl!

Mack: But does it make any
difference to *God?*

Arnie: If it does to me, it must
to *him* too!

*(Fade out on Arnie's smug
face.)*

"It's O.K. to Laugh in Church":
A Celebration

The leader(s) reads the line which serves as the heading for
each section of the service. Remember, like the services at the
close of every chapter, this is given only as a suggestion. Feel free
to change or adapt any or all of it. Some of the skits you have
created might fit in at various points.

I. "A funny thing happened to me . . ."
Call to Worship:

Leader—Ho, everyone who thirsts . . .

People (or each of the responses could be made by different
persons scattered through the congregation)—*Who*—me?

Leader—Yes, you. Come to the waters; and he who has no
money, come, buy and eat!

People—Hey, what sort of place is this—a bread line?

Leader—Yes, in a way, though our bread is the One whom we
call the Bread of Life. So, come, buy wine and milk without
money and without price.

WYUK: Channel 6
"A LAUGHING MATTER"

People—Now *that* sounds like a bargain!

Leader—Why do you spend your money for that which is not bread, and your labor for that which does not satisfy?

People—I don't know ... maybe because no one told us differently.

Leader—Listen closely to me and join in the party, it's "all in God's family," and you're invited.

People (all)—Right on.

Song: "Hey! Hey! Anybody Listening" or "We're Here to Be Happy"

II. "on the way to hell ..."

Act of Confession:

Share those things that make you or the world sad or unhappy. Or put together an audio collage of the awful things spoken by Ted Baxter, Lucy, Rhoda's mother, Archie Bunker, Gloria, Felix and Oscar, George Jefferson and his mother, and so forth. Write a congregational response to these.

III. "I met a man with a Cross."

The Assurance of Pardon:

Read passage(s) of forgiveness from the Scriptures: John 3:16; Isaiah 53; Romans 3:6-11; II Corinthians 5. And/or put together another audio collage of situation comedy characters forgiving one another.

IV. "He was dancing around it ..."

Act of Praise:

Sing the Gloria Patri or another short song of praise. If you have dancers in the group, they could interpret the song. Or make an audio collage of the opening theme songs of a number of sit-coms, and add slides of happy, celebrating people.

V. "and he said, 'Pilate and the priests, the guards and the crowds ...'"

The Scripture Lesson:

Read one of the Gospel accounts of the trial of Christ. Let one or more of the group comment on this, based on your discussion of Question 8. Or, if you have been taping any of the shows, use some of the scenes in which a character is acting self-important or putting on airs. Or, play "Herod's Song" from *Jesus Christ: Superstar.*

VI. "thought *they'd* had the last laugh. ..."

Meditation:

Read a Gospel account of the Crucifixion. Show slides of this—either as it is being read or set to the words of the

WYUK: Channel 6

"A LAUGHING MATTER"

Crucifixion scene from *Godspell* or *Superstar*. Mix in scenes of modern hurts and ills.

VII. "but I busted out of the grave . . ."

Affirmation of Faith:

Play or sing "Long Live God" from *Godspell*. Read one of the Easter accounts from the Gospels.

VIII. "and *now* who's the one that's laughing?'"

Benediction:

Sing "Lord of the Dance" or present a dance interpretation of this, concluding with everyone joining hands and singing in a circle.

Pass the Peace.

KNEW: Channel 7—

Man's News and the Good News: Fact and Faith

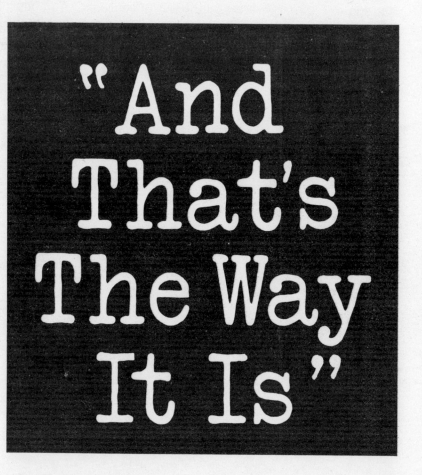

"*And That's The Way It Is*"

"And Now a Word from . . ."

For many years Walter Cronkite has concluded the "CBS Evening News" with the words that make up the title of this chapter. Few of us doubted his statement, except perhaps for Spiro Agnew and his minions. After all, we had *seen* the news, hadn't we? But is seeing always believing? Is that the way it is? Or is there more to the affairs of the world than meets the eye? I'm not just thinking about editing or managing the news (though this is an issue you might want

KNEW: Channel 7

"AND THAT'S THE WAY IT IS"

to consider), but something far more basic—the very nature of the way we perceive history, what some would call our faith-stance. The CBS camera-eye can record the external events of humanity and nature, but not their meaning. For this we have Eric Severeid. But we dare not rely on him alone. Thus in this session (or sessions) you are invited to probe together the nature of faith and experience, of sight and insight, and the claim that there is more to reality than meets the CBS eye. As Paul stated long ago, "What no eye has seen, nor ear heard, nor the heart of man conceived, what God has prepared for those wo love him, God has revealed to us through the Spirit."

For the Leader

1. If planning ahead was important for the other sessions, it is even more necessary for this chapter.

2. You *might* need: two extra TV sets, TV dinners.

3. Have on hand: cassette recorder and tape of "And Now a Word from ..." segments, Bibles, copies of this book, paper and pencils, Simon and Garfunkel's "Seven O'Clock News/Silent Night," news magazines, newspapers, transistor radios, and masking tape.

4. As the group gathers, play the song "Seven O'Clock News/Silent Night." You could record this on your cassette four or five times in a row so that it would be heard during your first few minutes of "gathering together time."

For the Group

1. Here are two possible ways of kicking off this session. Even if you or your leader choose the first, it would be a good idea to follow the suggestions of the second option. A few members closely observing the newscasts over a week might discover any pattern or emphasis of the newscast.

Option a. The group gathers early in the evening to watch the network newscasts together. Make this a supper party and serve—what else?—TV dinners. Have three TV sets on hand, each tuned to a different network (assuming that you can receive all three major networks in your area). Many in the group might want to scan all three newscasts simultaneously, but some members should volunteer to observe details of each network. Pass out paper and pencils for note-taking.

Option b. The group divides into three sections at the end of the previous meeting. Each agrees to watch the newscast on a particular channel for a week. All are asked to keep a log listing and describing the date, time and network, name of anchormen, the order of appearance for each story, and the time and nature of commercials. During the commercial breaks, while the facts are still fresh in your mind, jot down a brief summary of the news stories. How was each handled? What kinds of visuals are used—maps, on-the-scene reports, the faces of the newsmakers, interviews? Or is the newscast composed of mainly in-the-studio commentary? Are live reports from the scene used as the story is still unfolding? How much time is given each report? (Use a stopwatch or the sweep hand on your watch.) Are there any human-interest features or commentary?

2. Pass around copies of newspapers, news magazines, and a couple of transistor radios. The print pieces should be from the same week so as to cover the same events.

What is your major source of news—tv, radio, newspapers, or news magazines? For another way of putting this ask the question: Which of these, in the event of a crippling strike, would you miss the most? From which do you usually learn of a breaking story?

To vary the discussion a little, try this. Take four large sheets of paper and print "TV," "RADIO," "NEWSPAPERS," and "NEWSMAGS," one word on each sheet. Tape these up on each of the walls of your meeting room. The leader now asks the members to go and stand by the media sign which they think best completes the following statements:

(a) The medium which is the most reliable source of news is————.

(b) The medium which provides the greatest depth of reporting or helps me to understand the news events is ————.

(c) The medium which involves me, which makes me feel that I am present at the event is ————.

Between each statement, the participants should pick out another person, and the two of them share their reasons for their choices. If time permits, each of the four media groups could select a member to present their reasons to the other three groups.

3. If your group is very interested in editorializing or news-slanting charges against television, this exercise might interest you.

KNEW: Channel 7
"AND THAT'S THE WAY IT IS"

a. News can be slanted by choice of words. As you see the news film unfold decide whether the commentary is straightforward, or whether certain "loaded" words are used to describe the events and the people. Is the visual portion allowed to tell the story? Do you think that more words than necessary are interjected? Does the tone of the commentator's voice, his speed of delivery, his actual words match what you are seeing?

b. The film editor can control what you see. A rock concert might generally be a peaceful gathering, but he/she can select the more exciting scenes of a fight on the outskirts to show on "The Six O'Clock News." Or in our era of ecology, the aftermath of litter, especially if the concert was outdoors, might be emphasized. Hundreds of feet of film showing other aspects of the event will wind up in the discard bin.

c. The reporters at the scene might have sought out the opinions of many people, but only selected ones will probably be broadcast. Do you think that this fact will influence the person being interviewed, especially if he/she is speaking for a particular cause or viewpoint?

d. The very nature of a camera is to edit out everything that is not within range of its lens. Try this: hold your hands in front of your eyes and form a small rectangular frame with your fingers. Look through this at the people and objects around your room. Imagine that this is the viewfinder of a TV camera. Note how much is blocked out that you can see normally. Hold your "viewfinder" close to your eyes; you have the effect of a wide-angle shot. Move your hands farther away for the effect of a medium and a close-up shot. Note how little of the object is covered within the frame.

Remembering the TV audience will see nothing else but what your camera picks up, how can you depict the following:

—A peaceful demonstration which attracts a lunatic fringe bent on violence.
—A demonstration at which the police arrest the leaders and many of their followers.
—A women's liberation march or rally. The participants include a mixture of young and old women, married and single, even a number of men.
—A strike (of firemen, teachers, sanitation work-

ers, ———) which has continued for a long time with pickets confronting non-strikers and management personnel.

Divide into groups of four to six, choose one of the above, or make up your own, and work up two three-minute presentations of the story for "The Six O'Clock News"—one which is hostile, the other sympathetic to the persons involved. Describe what scenes you will show, and which you will edit out. Share these with the other groups.

One further word—news breaks fast, and deadlines are relentless, so charges of dark, sinister plots to manage the news are highly exaggerated. Errors do result from the necessary rush to finish a story by air time, and biases do surface, but these are usually honest errors, as can be found in any profession.

4. Divide into three groups. Imagine that you are a first-century A.D. news team. One team comes from each of these three groups:

Romans, Pharisees, and priests;

Disciples of Jesus;

Poor of the land.

KNEW: Channel 7
"AND THAT'S THE WAY IT IS"

Word has just come into your newsroom that Jesus of Nazareth has been arrested, tried, and condemned to be executed that very morning. It's a big story, so the producer/director have decided to give it from five to seven minutes of the half hour (minus seven minutes for commercials) of the Friday night news.

Each group should work up a two- or three-minute background story, then the story of the trial and execution. Describe what techniques—visuals, interviews, still photos, maps, types of camera shots, etc.—you would use in your telecast. If you have time, write out a script. Remember, the newscast should reflect the viewpoint of your group and your audience. Time your presentation with a watch. If possible, video tape each presentation; maps and large pictures could be borrowed from church school files.

Share your "telecast" with the others. After all have been presented, compare them as to emphasis, what was left out, what included. Do any present the whole picture? What view of Jesus would each audience receive?

5. Television is well-suited to capture the action and drama of public events. Indeed, the very presence of TV

cameras can intensify or even change the proceedings. But there are some events which, because of their nature, would not be as accessible to the eye of the camera. The Crucifixion would be a made-for-TV event, but what about the Resurrection? What would a camera crew pick up on that Easter dawn?

Let the same news teams that covered the Trial and Crucifixion now attempt to create a news story on the Resurrection. Your raw material is the four Gospel accounts and Paul's in the fifteenth chapter of his First Corinthians. Do you find any conflicts or discrepancies in the accounts? How will you reconcile them? Or will you?

"And Now a Word from . . ."

Because TV is a visual medium, it thrives on the specific and concrete. Faith, on the other hand, is concerned not only with the visible and material, but with the invisible—the encounter of a person with a nonmaterial God. Many of the great events described in picture-language in the Bible would not come across too well on TV, for they are faith-events. And "faith is the conviction of things not seen." Despite the crude efforts of film makers to depict the call of Moses, the real

essence is missed by their bumbling attempts to portray the Bible literally. The call of Moses is basically an internal event, the struggle of a fugitive shepherd with his conscience and his sense of the transcendent presence of God driving him back to his captive people. A CBS camera crew could record a shepherd climbing up a mountainside for a closer look at the spot where the sun's rays seemed to be reflected so brightly. Had they followed with a mobile camera unit, they would have seen Moses, sandles off, sprawled awestruck on the ground before an area where the sun's reflected rays seemed to be dancing around the branches of a bush. It would not resemble the phony asbestos creation of a DeMille film. This is not to say that the call of Moses is not real or factual. Of course it was, for it has changed the course of Hebrew history, and through that of the Western world as well. But the essence of the call was a faith encounter. A tape recorder might have picked up the rumblings of thunder or an earth tremor, but not the recognizable words of Exodus 3. This was in the realm of Moses' private experience, the realm of the poet and prophet, not of the news cameraman.

6. You might want to close with the long "And Now a Word from . . ." here. Or you can conclude with a discussion of the nature of fact and faith.

a. Describe "factual" or scientific knowledge. What does it depend on?

b. Describe "faith" or "revealed" knowledge. (You might want to look up "faith" in a Bible dictionary or concordance to see how the word is used in the Scriptures.) Compare these two ways of approaching reality. Are they at odds with each other, or can they go together? Do the biblical events belong to one or the other—or to both?

Close with a reading of portions of Hebrews 2 or with a hymn of faith, such as "Faith of Our Fathers" or "Hey! Hey! Anybody Listening?"

Further Probes

1. Marshall McLuhan claims that television has now made the world into a global village. Think back over the last ten or fifteen years and recall the effect some of these events have had on you due to TV. To get you started: the presidential inaugurations; the political conventions and election eve coverages; the NASA launchings and moon landings; the Olympic games; the

KNEW: Channel 7
"AND THAT'S THE WAY IT IS"

march on Washington; the assassinations of John F. Kennedy, Martin Luther King, Jr., and Robert Kennedy; the Vietnam war reports; the Selma march; the Watergate reports and hearings; President Nixon's resignation and farewell.

Share your reaction to one of these televised events.

2. Here are some additional biblical events which have influenced our tradition, but the essence of which would escape the TV camera. Divide into small groups and discuss them.

a. Genesis 12—the call of Abram. What would a tape recorder pick up? Was there an audible voice of God? Or might we see a man thrashing around on his pallet, unable to sleep, mumbling to himself, looking like a person in an Alka-Seltzer or Sominex ad?

b. Genesis 32—Jacob's wrestling match. Would this really compete with "Saturday Night Wrestling"? Could this be the author's way of picturing an inner struggle with the God of the patriarchs, a crossroad in Jacob's life leading to a whole new way of living and relating?

c. Exodus 19 and 20— Moses and the Ten Commandments. Is Cecil B. De-Mille's fiery finger zapping the tablets true to Scripture? Or would an ABC camera crew discover a half-starved prophet (remember how long he stayed on the mountain?) in a trance or deep meditation, occasionally chiseling away hurriedly at the stone tablets?

d. Some further incidents to explore in this vein are the temptations of Christ, the call of Isaiah; the Transfiguration, the Ascension, and the conversion of Saul—you can think of others.

"And Now a Word From . . ."

The above have been called "faith events" to separate them from the "facts" of the news reporter for discussion purposes only. The biblical events happened; they could have been reported on the evening news, but the claim that God was somehow revealing himself in these events could not be substantiated. Only faith, not a news camera, can testify to that. The external facts we can discover and see. The "faith fact" can only be revealed to us. This belongs more to the realm of an Eric Severeid than a Walter Cronkite. The Gospels, from the Greek, meaning "good news," are based on historic, provable events, but they are not unbiased reports. They are history interpreted through the Resurrection experience. They are advocacy journalism. They have a cause to promote, and they make no apology for this. They are written to convince the reader that Jesus is Lord.

3. For an excellent example of a "you are there" approach to the events of Holy Week, order the cassette "The Greatest Week in History" from Mennonite Broadcasts. This delightful series of four and one-half minute "newscasts" from Jerusalem covers each day's events—even including traffic and accident reports. Select portions of the tape for your group to react to. This will be useful for media projects also.

A Multimedia "Good News" Project

Choose a theme from Scriptures and such songs as Simon and Garfunkel's "Seven O'Clock News/Silent Night," "Patterns," "Richard Cory," "Bridge Over Troubled Waters," or the Beatles' "A Day in the Life," "Nowhere Man," "Penny Lane," or "Eleanor Rigby." Do you think the latter's death will be reported in "The Six O'Clock News"? Can you show how her life and death is as important to God as that of any famous statesman? Some further resources are Ray Repp's "Apple Pie," Kent

Schneider's "Liturgies of This Day," The Vanilla Fudge's "The Beat Goes On," *Jesus Christ: Superstar, Godspell,* and *Truth of Truths.*

Go through a good record collection, and you will find dozens of songs suggesting or relating to a theme. Other good sound sources are the documentary records obtainable at large record stores; especially useful is Columbia Record's *I Can Hear It Now/ The Sixties,* which includes all the sounds and voices that made news during that turbulent decade. After you select your songs, voice tracks, and Scripture passages, make a master tape. Make a copy of this for your work tape.

Buy one or more of the Super 8 Castle newsreels described in the special projects section of Channel 3. Cut out the useful scenes, arrange them in the order you wish, and splice them together. You can add your own film footage such as scenes of your town or city, close-ups shot from posters and pictures, even scenes from the network newscasts. For the latter, load your movie camera with high-speed Ektachrome movie film. You will pick up a "rolling" effect from the TV screen, but this won't be too bad in the short scenes that you will be using.

Gather together a stack of old *Life* and other news magazines to copy the pictures and ads with your slide cameras; also include old church school pictures and art prints for any biblical scenes you might wish to copy.

Different committees, after meeting together to plan the overall project, can then work on the separate components—the soundtrack, movie film, and the slides. If necessary, others can prepare a script for A-V and light cues. This could be an exciting project to prepare and present for Christmas, Lent, or Holy Week.

A Celebration of "Good News"

I. "And that's the way it is . . ."
Prelude:
   Play Simon and Garfunkel's "Seven O'Clock News/Silent Night."
Call to Worship:
   Good (morning, afternoon, evening), ladies and gentlemen. Today on the ——— O'Clock News we will be sharing these important stories: "God sends his Son to rescue the world." At this very moment Christians around the world gather to

KNEW: Channel 7
"AND THAT'S THE WAY IT IS"
Could you give us a quick summary for the 11:00 wrap-up?

KNEW: Channel 7
"AND THAT'S THE WAY IT IS"

celebrate this event. And also "God's people are sent out to declare this good news and to help mend a broken world." We'll be back with more of the details on these stories, but first an important message.

Song: "This Is My Father's World"

Act of Confession:

Leader—Yes, the wrong does seem "oft so strong," as we have reported many times. Hear again how in so many ways we have denied that "God is the ruler yet":

Option 1. Have someone during the preceding week tape the audio portion of the evening news each night. Select the highlights of four or five stories; use the voices of the people involved if possible (though each story segment should be no more than forty-five to sixty seconds so that your entire Confession is no longer than four or five minutes).

Option 2. Pick up the latest newspaper. Ask four or five people to choose and mark one of the stories of man's sin. Cut out the stories, number them in the order you want, and ask them to read just the headline and lead paragraph. After each segment or story, respond with "Good Lord, forgive us," or "Good Lord, save us."

Option 3. Create a slide interpretation of "We Beseech Thee" from *Godspell.*

Assurance of Pardon: Listen to God's Action News! You have been forgiven! Long before you could say "I'm sorry," God loved this world so much that he sent his only Son so that all who believe in him might not perish but have eternal life. Believe and accept the good news.

Act of Thanksgiving:

Sing the doxology, Gloria Patri, or a hymn of praise.

II. That's the way it was. . . .

The Ancient Word: Read from John's Gospel, chapter 1, or one of the other passages discussed in this chapter.

The Traditional Word: The Apostles' or Nicene Creed.

III. That's the way it ought to be. . . .

Song:

"In Christ There Is No East or West," "Not Alone for Mighty Empire," or "If I Had a Hammer"

Meditation:

Option 1. Show your multimedia; add your own comments or invite reaction and discussion.

"AND THAT'S THE WAY IT IS"

Option 2. Pull together some thoughts on the external and internal aspects of faith and the good news.

Option 3. Play "Liturgies of This Day" from Kent Schneider's excellent album *Celebration for Modern Man*. This would make a good soundtrack for a short multimedia or slide show.

IV. That's the way it will be.

Sharing Time:

Option 1. Let those who wish, share a story of something good that has happened to them recently.

Option 2. Ask several people to find articles about good news in the newspaper (or on TV) and share these.

Option 3. Have a prayer sharing time; let all who desire, offer prayer for the situations described in your confession, thanksgiving for any good news previously shared.

Song: "These Things Shall Be," "Peace My Friends" by Ray Repp, or "God Give Us Your Peace" by Phil West and Ed Summerlin

Charge:

And that's the way it is this (day of the week and date). Go now in God's name, remembering that you too are his messengers. By word and by deed proclaim the good news of a loving God who still loves this planet. In the name of the Father, Son, and Holy Spirit. Amen.

SIGN OFF

By now you should have explored a few aspects of television and the gospel. There are many other areas worth looking at together—TV quiz shows, violence on TV, the role of women in television, televised sports, religious programming. So go on and probe these also. And don't forget public television, too often an overlooked source of great entertainment, as well as of education.

There's much not to like on television—but there is much that is fine, beautiful, and moving. When you experience such moments, why not let the networks know this? They receive many critical letters, and deservedly so. But why not praise them also when they deserve it? You might help keep a good show on the air or encourage them to try other creative programs (and this is more risky). Here is a list of places to write:

ABC Television,
1330 Avenue of the
  Americas,
New York, New York 10019

CBS Television,
51 West 52nd Street,
New York, New York 10029

NBC Television,
30 Rockefeller Plaza,
New York, New York 10020

National Educational Television,
10 Columbus Circle,
New York, New York 10019

May you continue to watch creatively and critically, ever alert to the possibilities which this electronic marvel brings in exploring God's world and his good news.

Annotated Bibliography and Resource List

The following is by no means a complete listing of the materials available on the subjects discussed in this book. They are only suggestions as to where to begin to probe this vast mountain of literature.

Abrams, Nick, ed. *Audio-Visual Resource Guide.* 9th rev. ed. New York: Friendship Press, 1972.
  A very useful tool for locating films relevant to the topics discussed in this book.
Allen, Don. *The Electric Humanities.* Dayton: Pflaum/Standard, 1971. A very intriguing study of media; especially helpful in understanding the ideas of Marshall McLuhan.
Babin, Pierre, ed., *The Audio-Visual Man.* Dayton: Pflaum Press, 1970.
  Contains much practical information on producing media; also on the effects of media. Well illustrated.
Benson, Dennis. *Electric Evangelism: How to Spread the Word Through Radio and TV.* Nashville: Abingdon Press, 1973.
  This is a must for action-oriented readers; contains hundreds of ideas for local folk to become involved in mass media.
———. *Electric Love.* Richmond: John Knox Press, 1973.
  You will find many multimedia ideas here.
Coleman, Lyman and Curtis, Ken. *Festival.* Waco, Tex.: Creative Resources, 1973.
  A fascinating blend of small-group techniques and film-making.
Dalglish, William, *et al. Media III.* Dayton: Pflaum/Standard, 1973.
  The third volume of an invaluable set of books describing films, posters, records, and tapes.
Engstrom, W. A. *Multi-Media in the Church: A Beginner's Guide for Putting It All Together.* Richmond: John Knox Press, 1973.
  Especially helpful for those not too familiar with audiovisual equipment and its possibilities.
Jackson, B. F., ed. *Television–Radio–Film for Churchmen.* Nashville: Abingdon Press, 1969.
  Among many valuable features the brief history of broadcasting and the church's involvement is especially helpful.
Jones, G. William. *Landing Rightside Up in TV and Film.* Nashville: Abingdon Press, 1973.
  A programmed learning approach, often funny.

Bibliography

Kuhns, William. *The Information Explosion.* Camden, N.J.: Thomas Nelson, 1971.
Brief, well-written treatment of mass media. Good resource for leaders to have for background reading.

McLuhan, Marshall and Fiore, Quentin. *The Medium is the Massage: An Inventory of Effects.* New York: Bantam Books, 1967.
Heavy on visuals, light on text; good introduction to McLuhan.

———. *Understanding Media: The Extensions of Man.* New York: McGraw-Hill, 1964.
An old classic in this fast-paced era; basic, hard reading.

Marsh, Spencer. *God, Man, and Archie Bunker.* New York: Harper & Row, 1975.
A good example of media theology; includes excerpts from scripts.

Mead, Loren B. *Celebrations of Life.* New York: The Seabury Press, 1974.
If you were turned on by any of the worship suggestions, you'll love this collection of exciting celebrations.

Ralph, Barry L. *Can It: Using Resources Creatively in Worship.* Lima, Ohio: C.S.S. Publishing Company, 1975.
A very brief treatment of using media in worship.

Rynew, Arden. *Filmmaking for Children.* 5th rev. ed. Dayton: Pflaum/Standard, 1975.
Because of its intended audience it's also the best book for adults with no prior experience in this media.

Settel, Irving and Laas, William. *A Pictorial History of Television.* New York: Grosset & Dunlap, 1969. Well written and illustrated; nostalgia buffs will love it.

Valdes, Joan and Crow, Jeanne. *The Media Works.* Dayton: Pflaum/Standard, 1973.
Probably the most interesting probe of mass media in that it contains many projects and discussion ideas.

Woods, Richard. *The Media Maze.* Dayton: Pflaum Press, 1969.
A brief and inexpensive survey of mass media; would be helpful to have several copies of this on hand.

Young, Carlton R., ed. *The Genesis Songbook: Songs for Getting It All Together.* Carol Stream, Ill.: Agápe, 1973.
This fine collection contains several songs used in the suggested worship services including "Genesis One," "God Give Us Your Peace," "Happy the Man," "Hey! Hey! Anybody Listening?" "I'd Like to Teach the World to Sing," "If I Had a Hammer," "Morning Has Broken," "Peace, My Friends," "Sounds of Silence," "Take a Giant Step," and "We're Here to Be Happy."

For films about media write Mass Media Ministries; 2116 N. Charles Street; Baltimore, Maryland 21218.
Their newsletter is a good way to keep current on television.

For a copy of the tape about the last week in Christ's life, "The Greatest Week," write Mennonite Broadcasts, Inc.; Harrisonburg, Virginia 22801. Costs $5.00.

For valuable information about television from a Christian perspective, write the appropriate office of your denomination. The United Methodist Communications (475 Riverside Drive, Suite 1370; New

Bibliography

York, New York 10027), for instance, will gladly send information on such productions as their "Growing Spots."

Media Resources. For those turned on by the multimedia projects:

Blackhawk Films, Eastin-Phelan Corp.; Davenport, Iowa 52808.
A great source for Super 8 and 16mm films and slides. They issue a valuable monthly catalogue.
Castle Films, 404 Park Ave. S., New York, New York 10003.
A good source of 8mm films—newsreels, comedies, love and war stories, etc.
Edmund Scientific Corp.; Edscorp Bldg.; Barrington, New Jersey 08007.
Their catalogue includes many audiovisual supplies, weather balloons, etc.
Griggs Educational Services; Box 363; Livermore, California 94550.
Slide and filmstrip-making supplies listed.
Superior Bulk Film; 442-450 N. Wells St.; Chicago, Illinois 60610. A good source for film- and movie-making supplies.